SPEED
TRAINING

SPEED
TRAINING

**HOW TO DEVELOP YOUR
MAXIMUM SPEED FOR MARTIAL ARTS**

Loren Christensen

Paladin Press • Boulder, Colorado

Also by Loren Christensen:

Deadly Force Encounters (with Alexis Artwohl)
Extreme Joint Locking and Breaking
Far Beyond Defensive Tactics
Fighting Dirty (video)
Fighting Power
Gangbangers
Masters and Styles (video, with Mark Hatmaker and Vince Morris)
Restraint and Control Strategies (video)
Skid Row Beat
Speed Training: The Video
Surviving Workplace Violence
Vital Targets (video)
Warriors

Speed Training:
How to Develop Your Maximum Speed for Martial Arts
by Loren Christensen

Copyright © 1996 by Loren Christensen
ISBN 10: 0-87364-859-5
ISBN 13: 978-0-87364-859-2
Printed in the United States of America

Published by Paladin Press, a division of
Paladin Enterprises, Inc.
Gunbarrel Tech Center
7077 Winchester Circle
Boulder, Colorado 80301 USA
+1.303.443.7250

Direct inquiries and/or orders to the above address.

PALADIN, PALADIN PRESS, and the "horse head" design
are trademarks belonging to Paladin Enterprises and
registered in United States Patent and Trademark Office.

Visit our Web site at www.paladin-press.com

Table of Contents

Acknowledgments

As always, I want to give thanks to my family, who is always there, always supportive, and always a source of so much joy.

A special thanks goes to those instructors, students, and friends who assisted me in this project. To Gary Sussman, my senior student and photographer, for his excellent work behind the camera. The studio shots are all his work.

Thanks to the models who lent their time in front of the camera: Amy Christensen, Dan Christensen, Gina McGriff, Mark Whited, Gary Sussman, Kelli Sheffer, Geoffrey Steenson, Dan Anderson, Brian Vincent, Tim Delgman, Brian Grose, John "JT" Taylor, and Nader "Ned" Shatara.

I would like to give recognition to the following martial arts instructors who took the time to share with me some of their ideas and exercises on speed development:

Dan Anderson
Dan Anderson Karate
311 N.E. Roberts
P.O. Box 1463
Gresham, OR 97030

Tim Delgman
Zen Budo Kai of San Francisco
1711 Peach Place
Concord, CA 94518

Rick McElroy
McElroy's Martial Arts Academy
P.O. Box 22243
Hilton Head, SC 29925

Robert Pater
Shidare Yanagi-Ryu Aiki Jujitsu
P.O. Box 80222
Portland, OR 97280

Glen Smits
Eagle Martial Arts
131 Cragsmoor Road
Pine Bush, NY 12566

Introduction

Over the past three decades I have had the opportunity to meet and train with many top competitors and instructors. I have been impressed by some and disappointed by a few. When I have been disappointed by a martial artist, it has usually been because his skill failed to live up to his publicity. But when I have been impressed, it has *always* been because the martial artist possessed two factors: knowledge and speed.

Though most martial artists can accumulate knowledge, few can apply everything they know. Lots of them can talk about concepts, principles, and techniques but are unable to make them work when put to the test. I believe a true master is one who can demonstrate what he is talking about—and do so with great speed.

I am fascinated with speed in the martial arts. I've been in law enforcement since 1967 and have always tried to keep my personal training as street oriented as possible. I think tournament-style hook kicks to the temple are as useful as breasts on a snake, and I can't help but yawn at Jean-Claud Van Damme's leaping, spinning crescent kicks. Although over the years I have seen just about every fancy punch and flippy-dippy kick there is, the one ingredient of the martial arts that still thrills this aging scrapper is speed—hands that move as quickly as a serpent's tongue and kicks that crack the air like the lash of a bullwhip.

I once saw Bruce Lee at an East Coast tournament where he was a guest celebrity. He was giving a tournament fighter named Louis Delgado, who has since passed on, some tips on closing the gap and scoring with a backfist. I remember standing with my mouth hanging open in awe as Lee snapped out backfists so lightning quick that they were nearly invisible.

In the late 1980s I attended a seminar by Joe Lewis. Though by this time I had earned several black belts in three arts, after five minutes with Lewis I felt as slow as spilled glue. He moved like an actor in a flickering old-time movie: one moment he would be here, a split second later he would be there. Attempting to hit or punch him was like trying to punch a tornado.

Years ago, I saw Ed Parker hit a guy with controlled punches so many times within three seconds that there was no possible way I could have counted them. His blurred hands moved like the sticks of a crazed drummer, leaving no part of the poor guy's body unstruck.

There have been others. A Japanese foreign exchange student in college who could front kick with such velocity that I was never able to block it, even when I set myself and waited for it. The karate instructor who let you punch at him as fast and hard as you could and who then would flick out his hand, tap you three times on the forehead, and then block your punch. The arnis teacher who could whip you with his rattan stick a dozen times before you fully appreciated the sting from the first blow. And the jujitsu man who could dump you on your rear, painfully pick you up, and dump you back down before you realized you had been picked up.

Though there are a few exceptions, most top competitors and instructors agree that speed is one of the most important attributes a fighter can possess.

Physical strength, courage, flexibility, endurance, sparring ability, and grappling skill are all important, but if you are not fast enough to block your opponent's attack or you are too slow to hit him, the other attributes will be of little value.

Though volumes have been written on the other attributes, little can be found in the martial art books and magazines about ways to develop speed. The how-to article or book may go into great depth about a concept, a principle, or the mechanics of technique, but there is seldom anything written on how to improve the speed of a punch, kick, step, or block. In fact, I have seen entire volumes written on a particular fighting system without the author once mentioning the issue of speed. On those rare occasions when it is mentioned, it's only to say that the movements should be done quickly. But never does the author say *how*.

Instructors stand before their classes barking, "Pick it up. Come on; that's too slow. Faster, punch faster." Their commands are as useless as shouting, "Come on. Grow taller," because the instructors rarely, if ever, tell their students *how* to go fast.

There are a lot of students and instructors who have absolutely no idea how to increase speed. Most are under the impression that you either have it naturally or that it will develop over time.

Sure, a certain level of speed does happen with maturation, but are there ways a fighter can develop speed at a faster rate than just waiting for time to pass? Are there ways to make a slow person faster, or a naturally fast person even faster? Can perception be improved? Reflexes sharpened? Timing polished? Can weight training make muscles move faster? Are there shortcuts? Are there things that can be done to double your speed immediately? Yes, to all of these questions. And this book will show you how.

There are tournament champs who write books about how to stretch, bodybuilders who write about how to build big shoulders, and movie actresses who sell videos about how their special cream formulas keep them youthful. The marketing ploy is that if you buy these books and videos you too will be just like the authors: flexible, strong, and pretty.

The reality is that many of the people selling these products have been blessed with good genes and would have all these physical qualities even if they did no more than eat chocolate. For example, there is a guy who poses in stretching machine ads, conveying the message that he got his flexibility from the machine, though he could do the splits before he ever took his first karate lesson. I know one massive bodybuilder whose diet consists mostly of donuts and soft drinks, but he has gotten paid to lecture on the importance of eating correctly. I know another who has made tons of money selling articles on how you can build awesome calf muscles like his, though he had awesome calves before he ever touched a weight. And those aging actresses who peddle skin care products are so blessed with good genes they would still look youthful if their careers had been spent working in a coal mine.

The point of all this is to answer a question you might be asking about now, "Who is this guy Christensen, and what gives him the authority to write a book on speed?"

My martial arts history is simply this: I began studying karate in 1965 and though my emphasis has been on karate over the years, I have also studied arnis and jujitsu and familiarized myself with several other arts. I have a wall covered with blood- and sweat-spattered black belt certificates, but with all the 25-year-old "masters" running around, not to mention the "grand masters," "professors," and, oh yes, "doctors," I'll stay away from mentioning my degrees and titles. And though I was lucky enough to be ranked a few times in the "top 10" in kata competition in the 1980s, I'm most happy about surviving countless street confrontations in my capacity as a police officer since 1967.

Am I fast? Well (he said with great humility), I've gotten ten a few compliments. But I pale in comparison to the likes of Bruce Lee, Joe Lewis, Paul Vulnak, Al Decascos, and Larry Tatum. These guys, and many others, are my heroes. I want to be as fast as they are or were. Will I ever be? Probably not. But in spite of Father Time and all the old and new injuries, I'm going to continue to improve.

This book is a compilation of drills, exercises, concepts, and principles. Some I've made up over the years; most I've learned from instructors I've trained with and from reading. A few instructors were kind enough to respond to a questionnaire I sent out asking for their ideas on speed development. Their replies are found herein.

Although techniques, exercises, and drills are universal and no one can claim ownership, I've tried to give credit to people from whom I learned specific techniques. Some of the material herein has evolved by chance through my training, experimentation, and teaching, though it may have been in existence in another fighting system for a long time. To those martial artists who created a technique long before I "discovered" it on my own, I apologize for not giving you credit.

In writing this book, I thought of myself as a reporter as well as a martial artist. As a reporter, I researched as much as I could, given the time I allowed for this writing project. As a martial artist, I experimented with all of the exercises and drills. Some were great; some were good; none were bad. If I liked a drill or concept, I made it clear, but I refrained from commenting if I didn't, because I didn't want to prejudice your opinion against something that might work for you.

I have learned a great deal working on this project, and that from a guy who has been punching and kicking since 1965 (if it wasn't for a palm full of Excedrin tablets every morning, I'd have a pretty rough day). It has been a lot of fun, too. I've felt like a kid in Toys-'R-Us playing with all of these drills, and the exciting news is that I've gotten faster in the process.

Oh yes, I've awakened a couple of old injuries, so take a hint: don't get overzealous and try everything the first week. Know that you can't develop speed if you are tired or overtrained. It's better to choose one exercise from each category, such as one for perception, one for reflexes, one for hand speed, one for kicking speed, and one for closing the gap.

The book contains drills to practice by yourself and some to practice with one or more opponents. There are relaxation methods to reduce tension and muscle contraction so that your movements will flow unencumbered. A section on visualization and positive self-talk will help bring out speed from deep inside your subconscious mind. There are specific exercises you can do with weights to make the exact muscles involved in your punches and kicks stronger, and thus faster. And there are dozens of drills and exercises that will make you faster than you ever thought possible. Although I could not help but show my prejudice for street-oriented martial arts training, virtually everything in here relates to sport martial arts as well.

Allow me to comment on my use of certain terms. Though there are thousands of female martial artists training today, I chose to use the pronoun *he* throughout the book over the more awkward *he/she* or *s/he*. I also used *karate* as a generic term for all the punching and kicking arts at the risk of alienating all the students of kung fu, taekwondo, and jeet kune do. I thought the word *grappling* best described the fighting arts that use throws, joint locks, and leverage techniques. I took this approach for ease of writing and reading, as well as to keep the word count down. I pray I have not slighted anyone.

Writing this book was relatively easy compared to what you have to do. You have to get sweaty and tired— and you have to do it a lot because improvement takes time and effort. But it's definitely worth it because it's fun to be fast.

Instructor: "What do we want?"
Class: "Speed!"
Instructor: "When do we want it?"
Class: "NOW!"

The Elements of Speed

L et's take a look at the elements that constitute your ability to move quickly. It's important to be aware of these because you need to address each of them in your training in order to maximize your speed potential. Later, as you study the assortment of drills and exercises in this text, take note of which element is being worked.

REACTION TIME

Reaction time is the interval between your first perception of a stimulus to the moment when you begin a response. For example, when you are attacked with a backfist, your reaction time is from the instant you see it to the moment you begin to block or duck. To do this, your brain must (1) recognize the stimulus as a backfist, (2) recognize it as a threat, (3) consider all the possible responses, and (4) tell your muscles how to respond.

MOVEMENT TIME

Once you have narrowed your response options to just one, your muscles must put your response into motion. Movement time is measured from the point you begin to physically move to the point when that movement concludes. For example, the clock starts the instant your foot leaves the floor and stops the instant it makes contact with an attacker's abdomen or, depending on the circumstances, the moment it returns to the floor.

RESPONSE TIME

Response time combines the time it takes you to perceive a threat, choose a response, set that response into motion, and complete the motion. Here is how it works with a backfist attack. The clock starts when you first see the backfist rushing toward you. It continues to tick away while you recognize the backfist as a bad thing that will hurt you. The clock ticks while you choose a response: block, evade, hit first, or give up and hope to do better next time. If you choose to block, the clock ticks as you select which block and as you thrust your selection toward the backfist attack.

Here is where I humbly disagree with the scientific research that has been conducted in this area. Scientists say they have done considerable study in all three areas and have found that the greatest potential for reducing reaction time is with the last two areas: choosing a response and programming a response.

Now, I agree that proper training in choosing the right response to a stimulus will increase your speed, and I also concur that programming a response in your mind will improve your speed. In fact, this book is stuffed with drills, concepts, principles, and dirty tricks to do just that. But I also believe you can dramatically increase your speed to perceive, or identify, a stimulus, whether the stimulus is an attack or an opening you can attack.

One way to develop perception is through repetitive practice with a training partner. After thousands of repetitions, you will begin to recognize certain subtle cues indicative of a specific technique. You won't develop this ability from mindless practice, but from practice that involves careful observation on your part so that the way in which your partners punch or kick will be lodged in your subconscious mind. You will find several exercises in this book to help develop your ability to perceive.

I'm not going to argue the point with a white-jacketed scientist. Just give the exercises a try and find out for yourself.

Choosing a Response

Scientists found that when a subject had a number of options to choose from, response time increased. For example, if given a choice of five responses, the subject took longer to react than if there were only four. In fact, it was found that just doubling the number of options increased reaction time by roughly 150 milliseconds. Not much time you say? Consider that Muhammad Ali's jab could travel the full length of his arm in 40 milliseconds. In other words, if his jab was rushing toward your good looks and you had the option of two responses, your reaction would take nearly four times as long as his jab, and you could kiss that pretty face good-bye.

They did find, however, that response time can be reduced through practice. In one study involving two- and four-response exercises, the subjects showed that it took them longer to respond when there were four choices. But after they practiced—to the tune of 42,000 repetitions—their response time for the four-response exercises was the same as for the two-response ones.

Right to Right and Left to Left

There is one other aspect of making fast choices relevant to martial artists. Scientist conducted a test where subjects had to push keys when lights were turned on. When the left keys were arranged below the left lights and the right keys were arranged below the right lights, the subjects' response took only 17 milliseconds. However, when the keys to the left lights were placed on the right side and the keys to the right lights were placed on the left side, the subjects responded in about 150 milliseconds.

This strongly suggests that you might be faster blocking a strike to your right side with your right hand, rather than your left. Going back to the earlier example, if you blocked Muhammad Ali's jab to the right side of your face with your right hand, you just might maintain your good looks.

What Does All This Mean?

In a nutshell, all the scientific studies, not to mention just pure logic, tell us that the fewer choices we have to make, the faster our reflexes will be offensively and defensively.

As an example, let's consider the task of blocking kicks. There are schools that teach five different blocks for a front kick, four different blocks for a side kick, five different ones for a roundhouse, and so on. Is that really necessary? Are all these kicks so radically different that they necessitate different ways to stop or deflect their trajectory? The answer is a big, fat no.

Why should straight-line kicks, such as front, side, and back, require a different block for each? Why should round, hook, crescent, or any other circular kicks require a different block? The answer is, they don't. Sure, certain variations in a straight or circular kick will require you to modify the angle of your blocks, but there is seldom a need to completely change the type of block for every straight-line kick or circular type. Some fighters have even discovered that they can use just one block for all kicks—circular, straight, up, and down types. Granted, they have to torque their bodies or step off at different angles, depending on the type of kick and its trajectory, but the basic block stays the same.

Scientific studies on response programming has supported this concept. They have showed that an athlete is better off modifying an in-progress movement to deal with an unexpected event rather than attempting an entirely different movement. What this translates to is this: if you are expecting a front kick to your midsection but your opponent throws a lead-leg roundhouse, your chance of successfully blocking the surprise kick will be greater if you modify the same block you were going to use for the front kick rather than choosing an entirely different one.

Initially, a student should learn several different blocks for each type of kick. Then after he has had time to use them all, he should narrow his repertoire to just one for straight-line kicks and one for circular, choosing blocks that work best for him, given his height, weight, strength, and speed.

KISS

Keep It Simple Stupid. The simpler your response, the faster you will be. Scientific experimentation proves what is a logical assumption: simple responses are faster than complex ones. In other words, the less muscular action that occurs, the less time the action will take. For example, a simple snap-block against your opponent's jab is going to be much faster than back-flipping, landing in a split, and executing a double-palm strike to his thighs (no matter how many points this gets awarded in 1990s' kata competition).

Faking to Increase Response Programming

OK, now that you know that the fastest way to block your opponent's jab is with a simple response, can you use that information to slow your opponent's response programming? Sure.

First, know that when a stimulus is made more complicated, overall response time is going to be slower, such as when you throw a fake backfist followed by a reverse punch. But be careful not to throw the combination too close together. Studies have shown that if you throw the punch virtually on top of the fake, a person reacting will see the two attacks as one, and the fake may not have the desired effect. Likewise, if you are throwing a fake at the face of an intoxicated person, and even if you wait a beat before you throw the second punch, his numbed reflexes may fail to react to the backfist.

Because we are only talking milliseconds here, a time virtually impossible to measure in your training facilities, the best way to learn proper timing of a combination fake and punch is by practicing on a variety of opponents. That way, experience will determine what works most often on most people.

There has been considerable study in the area of reflex and reaction time, far too much for us to go into here. The interested reader can get a copy of *Sports Research Monthly Special Report: Minimizing Reflex and Reaction Time*, published in 1988 by the American Sports Research Association in Santa Monica, California.

By Any Other Name

In my research, I ran across instructors who at first glance, appeared to have broken down the elements of speed differently than I have above. Instructor-competitor Steve Sanders, a kenpo stylist who possesses awesome speed, breaks speed down into five areas: physical speed, natural speed, defensive speed, offensive speed, and mental speed.

In their book *Jun Fan/Jeet Kune Do: The Textbook*, Chris Kent and Tim Tackett divide speed into two basic categories: movement speed and reaction speed. Then, within each of these categories, they break the elements down even further.

Bruce Lee, in his book *The Tao of Jeet Kune Do*, lists five types of speed: perceptual speed, mental speed, initiation speed, performance speed, and alteration speed.

I could continue listing how various experts have broken speed into separate components, but it isn't necessary because they are all basically the same. They may be called by different names, but they all fall into one of the three categories listed above.

Working with What Our Parents Gave Us

A few pages ahead, we will take a brief look at fast-twitch and slow-twitch muscle fibers that determine to a great degree your natural potential for speed. But even if you are a martial artist cursed with a predominance of slow-twitch fibers, you will learn how to vastly improve your natural speed with the right exercises. On the other hand, if you were blessed with a predominance of fast-twitch muscle fibers (I'm so jealous, you rat), proper training will turn you into a speed demon.

Let's Get Busy

If you are to dramatically improve your overall speed, you must address all areas in your training. Admittedly, some are not as much fun or as interesting to train in as others, but you must nonetheless train in them all.

Look at it this way: if you think you are slow and you have not been training in, say, perception speed, that is probably the reason; on the other hand, if you have already developed good speed, but have yet to train in all areas of it, think how much faster you will be when you train comprehensively.

Developing a Strong Foundation for Speed

If a tree doesn't have deep roots and a strong trunk, its long limbs and beautiful leaves won't survive. In this section we will examine ways to develop a strong foundation upon which to build your speed. This is an area you should refer to over and over, no matter how advanced or how fast you become. Just as you will never become an expert in your chosen fighting art if you don't maintain strong basics, you will never reach your full speed potential, nor will you hold on to your hard-earned speed, unless you continuously refortify the foundation on which it's built.

We are going to examine two areas that make up this foundation: the mental and the physical.

THE MENTAL CONNECTION TO OUTRAGEOUS SPEED

Don't skip over this section thinking it's some kind of mumbo jumbo. It's not. There is a definite and powerful connection between your mind and body, and once you make that connection, you will never be the same again. Learning to relax and knowing how to talk to yourself will open a new and amazing world of improvement.

The Importance of Relaxation

The one comment I heard or read over and over throughout my research for this book is that to move fast, you have to be relaxed. Try this experiment: flex your arm as if you were trying to impress someone with your muscular biceps (if you don't have a muscular biceps, fake it). Tense it hard and then, without relaxing, pop out a backfist. This time hold your arm in the same bent position but don't flex your muscle. Maintain a loose fist and relax your arm from your fingertips to your shoulder. Now, throw out a backfist. Quite a difference, right?

For your arm, leg, or your entire body to move with great speed, there must be a sudden contraction of muscle fibers. That is to say, to propel your body, to move that kick or punch with great speed, the muscles must go from a relaxed state to a sudden contraction. However, when you are mentally and physically tense, a roadblock goes up because the muscles will already be in a partly or totally contracted state. Then when you command them to move quickly, which is really telling them to contract for you, they can't because tension has already beat you to it. But when your muscles are relaxed, meaning there are few muscle fibers in a contracted state, you are able to move faster because you can call into play more muscle fibers to contract.

Physical tension in a real fight or competition is often the result of mental tension; that is, your mind is occupied with fear and busy with thoughts of attack and defense. This is called *stopping* because the mind is focused on only one thing, as opposed to flowing freely and taking in the broader picture. When the brain is occupied, your response time will be slow because any messages attempting to get through must either take a circuitous route or wait for other messages concerning fear, attack, and defense to be cleared away. Either way, your response will be delayed.

You live in a tension-filled world. School, work, relatives, spouses, friends, bosses, motorists, bill collectors, health problems, and self-imposed demands fill you with stress and tension. When you are mentally and physically tense, your energy dissipates at an accelerated rate, your perception slows, your reflexes are sluggish, and your techniques move with all the speed of a tired slug.

You can tell with some people whether they are stressed by the way they look and act; whereas other people appear cool and calm as a cucumber though tension gnaws at their insides with razor-sharp teeth. You may not even know you are fighting internal stress and tension, and because you don't always know, the battle may be affecting your martial arts performance and on your health. The relaxation methods illustrated here will help you learn to relax mentally as well as release tension from your muscles. At first, the procedures will take several minutes to do, but with practice, relaxation will wash over you with little effort. In fact, you are going to learn to bring on the pleasing state of relaxation just by saying a single word.

Sound mystical? It isn't. It's simple and fast, and it feels good. And the more you practice, the easier it will be to bring on the relaxed condition, no matter how lousy your day.

The Exercises

Though there are many relaxation exercises around, I'm going to illustrate only three because they are quite easy to do and they will help you almost immediately. After a few days of practice, you may settle on one exercise, finding that your mind adapts nicely to the familiarity of the same exercise over and over. On the other hand, you may prefer to have a couple of exercises to choose from in case there are days you respond better to one than the other.

Always find time to practice relaxation exercises and to give yourself positive self-talk.

Blue Fog

Wear loose, comfortable clothes and find a quiet place where you will not be disturbed. Lie down on a bed or sofa and place a pillow under your head. If you have a bad back, take pressure off of it by placing a pillow under your knees and uncrossing your feet. Let your hands rest comfortably on your lower abdomen. If you have a tendency to fall asleep when you lie down, sit in a comfortable chair.

Close your eyes and allow your body to sink heavily into whatever you are sitting or lying on. Breathe in through your nose, drawing the air slowly and deeply into your lower abdomen. The inhalation should take about six seconds; hold it in for three seconds and then exhale to a count of six seconds. The entire cycle takes 15 seconds.

There is no strain in this procedure. If your inhalation only took three seconds the first time, that is OK, but keep practicing until it takes a full, comfortable six seconds to inhale and six seconds to exhale. By the second or third day, you will be able to time your breaths without looking at a clock.

After just a few breaths you will begin to experience a mild calming effect throughout your body. It will come over you like a wave, and if you are normally tense and stressed, this new feeling may alarm you. But it's OK. This pleasant sensation means you are beginning to relax. To accentuate this feeling, visualize your incoming breath as a cool, blue fog curling into your nostrils, tumbling and swirling down into your lungs, your abdomen, thighs, and feet. At the completion of the six-second inhalation, visualize, as you hold your breath for three seconds, the fog tumbling throughout your body, cooling and calming you.

Now slowly exhale, imagining the fog reversing its course, swirling and tumbling up and out of your body and out your nostrils. But this time the fog's red—the result of having collected fatigue, tension, anger, and frustration throughout your body. As you repeat the cycle, breathing in the blue fog and exhaling the toxic poisons, you will find yourself sinking deeper and deeper into a state of relaxation.

Progressive Relaxation

This method involves progressive and systematic relaxation of all the major muscle groups: neck, shoulders, arms, chest, abdomen, buttocks, thighs, calves, and feet. Your objective is to tense and relax each major body part until you are completely bathed in a wonderful sensation of total relaxation.

Assume a comfortable position on the floor or bed or in your favorite chair. As with the blue fog method, the room should be quiet and comfortable and your clothing should be loose. Repeat a few deep inhalations and exhalations to help get you settled into your position.

Start the exercise by thinking about your feet. See and feel them in your mind: your toes, arches, heels. Tense them as hard as you can, mentally and physically contracting every muscle fiber. Now, stop contracting them and let them relax as you exhale the tension from them. Feel and enjoy the pleasurable, soothing sensations in your feet.

Next, move up to your calves, visualizing every inch for a moment before you tense them as hard as you can for about 10 seconds. Relax the tension and again feel the sensation that sweeps over the muscles. *Free tip:* The calf muscles may be susceptible to painful cramping when tensing. If this happens or any other muscle cramps up on you, stop the tensing procedure and begin massage.

After you have enjoyed the soothing relaxation in your calves, move on up to your thighs, buttocks, abdomen, chest, neck, and face muscles. Repeat the same procedure with each muscle group as you did with your feet and calves: awareness, contraction, abrupt relaxation. If you have trouble relaxing, you may benefit by segmenting your body even further: lower back, forearms, hands, and various parts of your face, in particular your jaw and forehead where tension often causes pain.

Each body part should get about 10 seconds of tensing and about 10 to 15 seconds of relaxing before you advance to the next muscle group. Remember to breathe slowly and deeply as you proceed. It should not take more than 10 minutes to complete your entire body.

Neutral Bath or Hot Tub

This easy method of inducing relaxation is most pleasurable and can be done every day (or just on Saturday night if that's the only time you bathe). All you need is a warm bathroom and a bath tub filled with water of the same temperature as your body, 98.6°F. The procedure is simple: you immerse yourself in the water and then lie back and let the warmth lull you into a relaxed state.

A neutral bath works because of the way the nerve endings on your skin surface reacts to stimulus. Many of the skin's nerve endings are cold receptors, and, when exposed to water colder than your body, will bring on goosebumps, shivers, even shock. On the other hand, water the same temperature as your body will have a soothing effect on the nerve receptors and overall nervous system.

Pick up a good thermometer at any pharmacy to make sure the water temperature is maintained at 98.6°. The air temperature in your bathroom should be warm enough so there is no cool air on your skin's nerve receptors.

You can use a hot tub, just make sure the water is 98.6°. Since mine is outside and I can't control the air temperature, I have to dash through the winter cold to get into my house. But I immediately take a warm shower and put on warm clothes, so I lose little of the effect of the warm soak.

Years ago before tranquilizers, a neutral bath was used to calm agitated mental patients, sometimes for several hours at a time. But you don't need to lie in the water that long. Try it for about 30 minutes at the end of your school- or workday or whenever you feel the need for the relaxing, sedative effect it provides. Though you may choose to have a neutral bath every day, you should never have one prior to a workout. The heat will drain your energy, leaving you wiped out halfway into your training. But if you are tense from your day and you just want to have a short, solo speed workout, hop in the neutral bath for a few minutes first. The tension will dissolve, and your speed drills will be more beneficial.

There are many other relaxation exercises, so if the ones illustrated here don't suit you, find a book or an instructor to teach you alternative ones. (My earlier book *The Way Alone* contains additional information on relaxation.) When you have found a method that suits you, practice it once or even twice a day. Eventually, as you become adept at self-induced relaxation, you will be able to bring it on easily and do it unnoticed just about anywhere at any time (the exception being the neutral bath, of course). You can relax while standing in line at the grocery store, sitting in a meeting, or idling in traffic. You don't always have to go into a deep state of relaxation, just far enough to experience the wonderful, soothing sensation. To practice self-suggestion, however, you will have to go deep.

Self-Suggestion for Greater Speed

We are all susceptible to suggestion, whether it comes from an outside source such as advertising or from messages we tell ourselves. When you practice self-suggestion, the cues come only from you and are heard only by you. The expression "you can talk yourself into or out of anything" sums up what self-suggestion is all about. With it, you can effectively influence both your thinking and your behavior.

Talk to Yourself

Martial arts instructor Glenn Smits in Pine Bush, New York, teaches his students the power of self-suggestion, or what he calls neurolinguistic programming. This is a process whereby you tell yourself over and over that you are becoming faster. By vocalizing positive thoughts, the subconscious mind is fed information that it believes is true. In time, your subconscious will begin to direct your body to act as it has been programmed: to move fast. There is nothing mysterious about this. It's simply the natural relationship between your conscious and subconscious mind.

Do it in the following way. As you go about your day, tell yourself often that your fighting techniques are getting faster and faster. Get specific: "My backfist is as fast as a bullet," "My side kick shoots out in a blur." Say these positive statements out loud when you are alone and silently when you are around others.

Leave yourself a Post-it note on your bathroom mirror with the message: "My roundhouse kick is faster today than it was yesterday." Put one on your dash, on your bedroom dresser, on your refrigerator. In time, the message will sink in, and your subconscious mind will believe it and direct your body to act it.

Let's get a little more complex now and look at how you can implant this message deeper into your subconscious mind. This requires you to be in a deep state of relaxation where your subconscious will absorb your programming more easily.

The Procedure for Self-Suggestion

Though the following procedure may look involved, it's really quite simple and will become even simpler the more you do it. In fact, you will probably become enthusiastic about the process and use it to improve other areas of your martial arts besides your speed.

The first step is to know exactly what you want to implant. Since we are talking about speed development, make a "want list" that reads something like this:

- When I train, I want to be relaxed so that my hand techniques, kicks, blocks, and body maneuvering will be faster.
- I want to be able to induce relaxation easily and on command.

Though these two wants are closely related, the process will be most effective when you work with just one goal at a time.

Find a comfortable, quiet place and use one of the exercises illustrated earlier to induce a deep state of relaxation. Take your time and go as deeply as you are able. As before, you want to bring on a wonderful feeling of warmth and an almost indescribable sensation that some people call letting go. Now that you are relaxed from the relaxation procedure, you talk yourself into an even deeper state. The following dialogue can be said silently or, if you have trouble concentrating, try mouthing the words or even saying them out loud. Use your own words and way of speaking. Repeat significant words and phrases. This is how I do it.

Now that I am deeply relaxed I will breathe in deeply and exhale slowly as I count slowly to

10. As I say each number, I will feel myself sinking deeper and deeper and growing heavier and heavier. One, I am sinking deeper into my chair . . . Two, I am growing heavier and more relaxed . . . Three, my eyelids are growing so heavy . . . Four, I'm sinking . . . deeper . . . Five, my eyelids are closing . . . Six, my eyelids are so heavy . . . Seven, I'm so heavy . . . Eight, my eyelids are closed . . . I'm so relaxed . . . Nine, I'm more relaxed than I have ever been . . . Ten, I'm completely, deeply relaxed.

Sometimes it will take 15 minutes to get completely relaxed; whereas other times it may take only five. It doesn't matter how long it takes as long as you reach that wonderful stage of deep relaxation.

Once you are there, enjoy the feeling for a few minutes before you move on. Sometimes it might feel as if you are on the edge of sleep, but your mind will be clear and alert, and your subconscious will be ready to receive self-suggestion.

The Tingling Hand Test

You are now going to conduct a simple test to determine how susceptible you are to the power of suggestion. You have already achieved a deep state of relaxation, so stay exactly where you are. Fix your eyes on a small object at eye level, such as a spot or tack on the wall in front of you. Your objective is to feel a mild tingling in one of your hands.

Talk to yourself this way.

I'm completely relaxed. As I slowly count to 10, and even before I get to 10, I'll experience a tingling or numbness in my right hand. One, I'm concentrating on my right hand . . . I can see it in my mind . . . it's completely relaxed . . . Two, I'm beginning to feel a pleasant tingling sensation in my hand . . . Three, I can see my

> hand in my mind's eye . . . it's relaxed . . . limp .
> . . heavy . . . relaxed . . . Four, I'm relaxed . . .
> Five, my hand is beginning to tingle . . . tingle
> . . . Six, it's a pleasant sensation . . . I'm relaxed .
> . . I feel heavy . . . my hand is tingling . . . Seven,
> it's tingling more now . . . it's becoming stronger
> . . . it's an enjoyable sensation . . . Nine it's real-
> ly tingling now . . . tingling . . . tingling . . . tin-
> gling . . . I'm now in a suggestible state and
> receptive to suggestions.

If you don't experience the tingling the first time you try, continue with the exercise as if you do. That way you will not waste the moment and will become smoother with the procedure. It's probably not happening because you have not reached a deep enough state of relaxation. It's important to concentrate hard on what you are doing and *believe* that the tingling will happen. Remember, this is all about autosuggestion.

Now that you are relaxed and have successfully tested your level of suggestibility, you are ready to proceed with the other suggestions. The tingling in your hand, howev-er, should be stopped so you can proceed without any dis-tractions. Use the following suggestions.

> The tingling in my hand will now go away
> . . . My hand will return to normal . . . I realize I
> have reached a deep suggestible state . . . My
> entire body is relaxed . . . Every muscle is
> relaxed . . . I like the sensation . . . The tingling
> in my hand has stopped . . . I'm now ready to
> receive suggestions in my subconscious mind.

Programming Your Subconscious Mind

Relaxed, you will now begin to talk to yourself. ALWAYS use positive statements and positive singular words; negative statements, such as "I am too tense," release negative energy and may bring on even greater stress and tension. On the other hand, positive sentences will release positive energy.

It's also necessary to form all your sentences in the present tense. "I am relaxed as I spar in class." "I am relaxed as I spar the black belts." Even if you are going to spar Brutus the Karate Killer a week from now, keep your statements in the present. "My arms are weightless, and my legs are weightless as I spar Brutus. My movements are quick and fluid because my muscles are relaxed."

As you feed your subconscious mind positive suggestions, continue to tell yourself that you are relaxed. "My kicks are lightning quick . . . I'm so relaxed . . . my hand techniques are fast, because I am relaxed . . . weightless."

Your subconscious mind likes powerful adjectives that form dramatic images. For example, use terms like lightning quick and explosive punches.

Continue to feed yourself strong, positive statements for about five minutes. When you finish, it's important to always come out of deep relaxation because you don't want to walk around in a highly suggestible state. Say something like this:

> In a moment I'm going to count slowly from five to one, and on the count of one I'll be fully awake, refreshed, alert, and responsive to my suggestions . . . Five, I'm beginning to return to normal . . . Four, I'm awakening . . . Three, I'm awakening . . . my eyelids are starting to open . . . Two, my eyes are open . . . One, I'm fully awake, refreshed, and responsive to my suggestions.

After you return to your normal consciousness, sit quietly for a few moments and enjoy the feeling of peace that has enveloped you. You may feel a lightness in your body as if your arms might drift upward. There is a clarity and calmness in your mind, and you will have greater control over it because there are fewer rambling thoughts bouncing about. It's a wonderful feeling; pause and enjoy it.

Keyword

This a quick way to achieve relaxation by using a specific word to cue your mind. I use my middle name, Wayne. It works well for me because I rarely hear it and I use only the middle initial when I write my name. Here is how it works.

After you have achieved a state of relaxation and suggestibility, tell yourself that every time you utter your specific word, you will begin to move into a condition of deep relaxation. Tell yourself this at the beginning of your autosuggestions, again in the middle, and once more before you conclude. You may need to repeat this each session for awhile until the word begins to work for you.

I use the keyword a couple of different ways. First, I use it to speed up the relaxation process when I practice my autosuggestion exercise. I sit in my chair, get comfortable, and then say the word. Immediately I begin sinking into relaxation. Then all I have to do is encourage myself to go deeper into it.

I also use it when I'm feeling tense. Sometime I say my word on the freeway when I am en route to something I am nervous about, such as a seminar. As the wave of relaxation overtakes me, I tell myself that I will be alert in my driving. For safety reasons, I don't allow myself to go deep, especially if I am tired or sleepy at all; I do it just enough to bring on a little relaxation to take the edge off.

I always use my word when I am getting ready to give a talk before a group of people, not only to relax, but to program myself to give a dynamic, flawless presentation.

Self-suggestion is a wonderful device that works. And because it's all done in your mind, it can be your little secret.

Sweatless Practice

Sweatless practice is the act of mentally visualizing a specific activity, whether it be a single punch or kick or multiple movements, such as in kata and sparring. To benefit from these moving mental pictures, you must call up all the details of the activity—sound, color, emotion, and speed—in utmost clarity, from the beginning of the sequence to its end. Your images must be so vivid, so real, that you feel as though the visualized activity is actually occurring. Kenpo instructor John La Tourrette, an advocate of visualization to enhance martial art speed, stated in the October 1994 issue of *Blackbelt* magazine, "If you can see it [in your mind], you can do it."

There have been numerous studies conducted showing the similarities between mental and physical practice. They have shown that people who physically practice an activity and those who practice it only in their minds for the same amount of time improve to nearly the same level. Champion athletes such as golfer Jack Nicklaus, tennis player Chris Evert, and karate great Chuck Norris all swear by sweatless practice.

I won Grand Champion in black belt kata one time with a kata I had practiced only with visualization. For four weeks prior to the tournament, I practiced the kata in my mind several times a day, while at the same time I put all my physical energy into practicing a weapons kata. I did my sweatless practice with such clarity in my mind and with such fighting spirit that at times I actually broke out into a sweat. The day of the event, I entered the division having practiced the form countless times in my mind. I won the division and went on to win the overall. I didn't even place in weapons kata.

Get Relaxed Again

As with self-suggestion, your mind is more receptive to visualization when you are physically and mentally relaxed. One of the best times to bring on the relaxed state is when you awaken in the morning or just before you go to sleep at night. Since your body and mind have just rested or you are preparing to rest, you are especially receptive to deep relaxation and visualization. But if you find yourself nodding off before you get to the exercise, sit up or move to a chair. It's important to always keep your spine straight whether you are sitting or lying.

Once you have induced deep relaxation, see yourself in your fighting stance ready to launch a blur of techniques, say a roundhouse-backfist-reverse punch combination. See everything clearly in your mind: your arms on guard in front of you, your chest expanding and contracting faster than normal, your feet shuffling about. And feel everything: the lightness of your arms and fists, the energy surging through your chest and abdominal muscles, the rough edge of your pant cuff against your ankles, and the weightlessness of your leg muscles.

Before you actually begin to visualize movement, know this: your visualization of a physical act must take the same amount of time as it would in reality. If you want to do a combination in one-quarter of a second, you must visualize it in one-quarter second. Explode! See and feel your rear leg step up and your front leg snap a belt-high roundhouse kick, followed by a whipping backfist before the kicking foot sets back on the floor, and concluded by a driving reverse punch as the backfist retracts.

How did you do? Bet you did it faster than ever before and with flawless form (only mentally disturbed, self-destructive people see themselves doing a technique slowly and sloppily, losing their balance and falling on the floor).

Head Swapping

Head swapping is a mental game in which you picture yourself performing a technique in place of someone whose speed you admire. It might be your instructor, the class senior black belt, or a colored belt with an exceptionally fast double side kick. It doesn't matter who it is because you are just going to borrow that person's head for a few minutes.

Let's say you are impressed with a female green belt's double side kick combination that she can do with perfect form and faster than a speeding locomotive. You have watched her many times as she first throws one, retracts it to bounce off the floor, and then fires out another. You think her double kick is great, and you want to be able to do it, too. You can, but first you have to cut her head off.

Begin by clearly picturing her in your mind: she is standing in her fighting stance, wearing her uniform, her green belt tied around her waist. Now, just like in the movies when a wispy, evil spirit enters someone's body, mentally superimpose your body over hers. When the merging is complete you move as one. Mentally see and feel every aspect of the two kicks as if you were she.

A slight variation is to imagine you are inside her head, looking out. As she executes her beautiful side kick, you see it as if you were looking at it with her eyes. Her movements are yours. It's weird but effective.

Let's have a reality check here. If you were born with a preponderance of slow-twitch muscles and you are head swapping with someone whose great speed is partly a result of being blessed with a preponderance of fast-twitch muscles, you will never, in reality, be able to attain that person's speed. However, head swapping will dramatically improve your speed because your body will stretch to meet what your mind is visualizing.

Many top instructors teach the value of sweatless practice.

Sensei Tim Delgman, a jujitsu instructor at Zen Budo Kai of San Francisco, says this: "As often as you can, visualize the correct, flowing, and smooth motion of your technique. Use visualization to analyze every aspect of your technique; pay attention to even the slightest detail."

Instructor Glenn Smits is a strong advocate of the mental/physical connection. "You must *see* yourself executing combinations faster and faster."

Tournament champion Keith Vitali used visualization to develop a winning attitude that helped rocket him to number one in the country. "I believe that the best compliment given me throughout my career was not about how fast I was or how good my kicks looked, but that the confidence I displayed and the look I had made everyone think I was going to win."

When Aboe Hada, World Karate Association bantamweight champion of the United States, was asked what made him different from the other contenders, he said. "Every time I punch the bag I am screaming to myself, inside my own head, 'I will be champion,' over and over. When I punch the bag, when I spar, all the time I say this to me; that is the difference."

Try deep relaxation, autosuggestion, and visualization and see what it does to your speed.

DAILY MENTAL TRAINING CHECKLIST

- Keep your mind firmly fixed on your goal of increased speed.
- Use visualization every chance you get.
- Tell yourself throughout your day that you are already fast and getting faster.
- Understand how every speed exercise helps you.
- Set big goals for yourself but use smaller ones as stepping stones to your success.
- Never quit trying. Starting means you are just half finished.

Your punches and kicks will never be fast without fast hip rotation. Mirror practice is essential. One way is to place your hands on your hips and assume a forward stance with your upper body turned away.

As you snap your hips forward, your arms and shoulders will also snap forward. Make sure your hips rotate first, not your arms.

THE PHYSICAL CONNECTION
TO OUTRAGEOUS SPEED

We have just examined specific mental exercises necessary to develop a strong foundation on which to build your speed. Now let's look at the physical elements.

The Importance of Fast Hip Rotation

Speed comes from all kinds of places, and to a new student and maybe even a few veterans, it may not make sense that doing something with your hips will make your fists move faster. It's commonly believed that the purpose of rotating the hips is to help give power to punches and kicks. This is true, but because the hips work like the drive shaft of a wheel, they create a larger and faster movement at their outer surface, thus increasing the velocity as well as the snap of a technique.

Though it's not the most exciting training exercise, you will be rewarded for your efforts with greater power and greater speed, and all it takes is 5 to 10 minutes per training session. Proper hip rotation is so important that many instructors consider its mastery the starting point of karate.

The mirror is your best friend because it will show you if you are rotating your hips properly. There are three ways you can visually check to see if you are rotating enough. With all three you begin in the forward stance, say with your left leg forward and your right hip rotated back to the right. The first method is to put your hands on your hips so that your left elbow is pointing virtually to the front, and your right elbow is pointing behind you. When you snap your right hip forward, your right elbow wings forward, stopping when both elbows are aligned to the front.

The second way is to hold a staff behind your lower back, so that the left end is pointing forward, with the right end toward the rear. When you rotate your hips, you can watch to see if the right end snaps forward to where both ends are even with the rear.

Make sure you are not turning your elbows or the staff first and your hips last. You want to rotate your hips first, so that they are rotating your elbows or staff forward.

The third way is to watch your belt ends. If you are not rotating your hips enough or are doing so too slowly, your belt ends will simply hang limply when you rotate. But if you are snapping your hips forward with good speed, your belt ends will flip about.

The next step is to work to coordinate your hip rotation with your punches and kicks. The final stage is to push the speed of this coordination.

With lots of repetitious practice and supplemental abdominal conditioning—fast hip rotation requires strong front and side stomach muscles—you will be well on your way toward success. Althoughattaining top speed in hip rotation won't happen overnight, it will eventually if you persist.

Free tip: If you have not worked on your hip rotation to any great extent, take it easy at first. If you start out with 20 hard minutes of hip snapping, you will be moaning and groaning the next morning as you struggle out of bed with an aching lower back. Don't snap your hips as hard as you can the first three or four workouts. After your muscles have been conditioned, then start pushing for speed.

Hip Tilt

This is somewhat similar to the knee-bend thrust technique discussed later in the section "Creating the Illusion of Speed" in that it provides you with a few additional inches of reach compared to the regular hip rotation. These additional inches will surprise your opponent because he won't expect you to be able to reach him. The hip tilt will also add power, speed, and snap to your punch. It works like this.

Assume your fighting stance, left leg in front. The first few times you try this move, do it without stepping forward, as if your opponent is close enough to hit without the step. Now, as you rotate your hips, tilt them forward as well and bend your knees a little. Think of it this way: there are water spouts on each hip, and you have to tilt your hips in order to pour the water out. Time the hip rotation/tilt/punch so that they all stop at the same moment. To coordinate the hip movement with a lunge, you must launch your punch first, scoot your lead foot forward, and rotate and tilt your hips (later we will examine the importance of launching the punch before you move your body). Speed comes from driving off your rear leg as you thrust your front foot forward. Since you have to move your entire mass across the space between you and your opponent, you lose much of the element of surprise that exists when you punch using just the hip tilt without taking a step. Nonetheless, when the entire movement is put together, your punch will be fast, and the forward momentum will give you power.

Weight Training

In my 30 years of teaching martial arts, I have observed that students who incorporate weight training with their fighting art are better students. As is the case with martial arts training, lifting weights helps them become more aware of their bodies: they have a greater understanding of how their muscles work, what it means when their muscles feel good or bad, and an understanding as to when they can push their training and when to slack off. As far as improving speed, training in progressive weight resistance helps them grow stronger so that they are able to exert greater speed and power when pushing, pulling, grabbing, kicking, jumping, and throwing.

In this day and age, it is hoped that there are not martial artists out there who still hold antiquated beliefs that weight training is bad for their performance. Twenty-five years ago there were many opponents of weight training. They advocated abstinence from barbells and dumbbells because they believed such exercises would injure joints and slow movement. Apparently they didn't ask Mas Oyama, the kyokushinkai master who used to beat bulls to death with his fists. He lifted weights for years and, in fact, favored the bench press, which he performed every day to the tune of 150 to 200 repetitions with a 170 barbell.

Then around 1970, prejudice against weight training began to change. At that time two physiologists at Springfield College in Massachusetts, tested 300 weight lifters and 300 people who did not lift weights. Both groups were asked to crank a single-arm machine that measured the speed of their arm movement. The result: the 300 students who weight trained could move the lever much faster than the 300 who didn't lift. Other studies were conducted that proved conclusively that weight training increased the speed of muscular contraction.

Speed is directly related to physical strength. A stronger muscle can more easily overcome resistance to movement, whether the resistance is gravity, tight clothing, or a powerful push from an opponent. Strong leg muscles can kick faster, and strong arms can more quickly wield a bo, a nunchaku, a sai, a kama, arnis sticks, or a sword.

I'm talking about reasonable muscle mass here. Arnold Schwarzenegger and Lou "Incredible Hulk" Ferrigno are never going to move quickly because their inflated bulk is too restrictive. On the other hand, Bruce Lee developed a lean muscular physique and could move his hands and feet at an incredible speed.

The effect of weight training is limited to what your mother and father gave you; it won't turn you into a Bruce Lee if you have not been blessed with his super genetics, such as the right ratio between fast-twitch and slow-twitch muscle fibers. But you can still improve, and as you do, you will move closer and closer to your highest capability. Again, this may not be the same as Bruce Lee's capability, but you will progress to a level that may mean the difference between first and second place in competition or, more important, the difference between surviving and not surviving in a real fight.

Fast-Twitch and Slow-Twitch Muscles

This could be a complicated subsection, but it won't be for two reasons. One, I can't get complicated because I'm just a simple lay person, not a doctor. Two, for our purposes here, we don't need to get complicated. So, to the physiologists among you, I apologize for the oversimplification of my description of muscle fibers, but simple is just the way I think.

We all have two types of muscle fibers, slow twitch and fast twitch, each requiring specific exercises to maximize their potential. Fast-twitch muscles have greater strength capacity, while slow-twitch muscles have greater endurance capacity. *Twitch* refers to how the muscle fiber responds to electrical impulses sent from the spinal cord. Again, this gets rather complex, and I encourage you to research it further if you are so inclined.

The leg muscles of world-class endurance runners contain 75 to 90 percent slow-twitch fibers, while sprinters have 80 to 90 percent fast-twitch muscle fibers. (What percentage of fast-twitch muscles do you think Bruce Lee had?) The only difference between men and women (in this regard, anyway) is that the muscle fibers in males are larger.

Each of us has a different ratio of fast-twitch and slow-twitch muscles. Scientists believe the number you possess of each determines your strength and speed potential. So how can you tell which way you are endowed? One way is to recall which sport you excelled in as a kid. If you were best at endurance activities, such as hiking, marathon running, and soccer, you probably have more slow-twitch muscles. But if you were good at activities that required quick, explosive speed, and power, like baseball, football, and sprint races, then you probably have more fast-twitch muscles.

Here is another way to determine what you have. If you presently have little endurance but tremendous speed, your ratio leans toward fast-twitch muscle fibers. But if you are not fast but have lots of endurance, you have a higher percentage of slow-twitch muscles.

Those fortunate individuals who begin their martial arts training already possessing great speed are people who have a greater number of fast-twitch muscle fibers. So what about us poor slobs who have an equal number of fast-twitch and slow-twitch muscles, or a preponderance of slow-twitch ones? Is there any hope for us in the martial arts?

Yes. Even if you are jammed full of slow-twitch muscles, you can greatly improve your overall strength and speed through weight training—proper weight training—along with the many exercises and drills illustrated in this book.

Separating Speed and Endurance Weight Training

As a martial artist, no matter what your fighting art, you need endurance and speed, which means you need highly conditioned slow-twitch and fast-twitch muscle fibers, both of which can be developed through weight training. But combining the two types of exercises may not be the best way to train. Sure, there are some individuals who have developed great physical strength, speed, and endurance through weight training, but they could have developed even higher levels of each if they had focused their training on one thing at a time.

What this means is this: when you are in the gym, spend your time training to increase your strength and speed, not your endurance. Let your muscular and aerobic endurance develop through activities such as practicing high reps, karate sparring, judo randori, and weapons kata.

Success with such movements as the backfist, side kick, and hip throw depends on a single maximum muscular effort executed in a split second. Specific weight-resistance exercises have the greatest positive impact on these so-called single-rep, maximum- effort movements.

For our purposes here, martial arts training is considered a single-rep endeavor. Granted you execute more than one throw during a judo workout, and throw more than one kick during a karate sparring session, but there is a break in between the movements where your muscles are allowed to recharge their strength. On the other hand, marathon running is anything but a single-rep activity. In fact, a two-hour race adds up to 20,000 sequential reps, called strides in the running game.

Specificity of Training

Specificity of training refers to weight training exercises that mimic the movements of your art. To explore the possibility, you must first examine a specific technique as to what muscles are involved, what track it takes, and the direction of the technique's return, if there is one. Once you understand the totality of the move, then research the myriad of resistance exercises to see what is most appropriate to your needs.

You will happily find that there are resistance exercises that mimic a few of your fighting techniques perfectly. On the other hand, there are many martial art movements that currently have no weight training equivalent, as least as far as the total movement is involved. So what do you do? Well, if you have the money and know a clever engineer, you can design specific pieces of equipment to mimic specific movements. But if you lack the cash, all is not lost.

Basic Weight-Training Exercises

The basic resistance exercises on the facing page will strengthen and develop speed in the muscles noted in the right-hand column.

These exercises should not be performed in circuit training fashion, that is, one after the other with no rest in between. Though it is an excellent way to develop cardiovascular fitness, that is not your purpose here. Your objective is to develop your muscles so that they have greater contractability, which will in turn increase the speed of your techniques.

Do three to five sets of 6 to 10 repetitions of each exercise with 30 to 60 seconds rest between each set, and two to five minutes rest between each body part.

BASIC RESISTANCE EXERCISES

Exercises	Muscles Worked
Bench Press	Punching Muscles
Bent-Over Dumbbell Rowing	Punching and Snap-Back Muscles
Squats	Kicking Muscles
Stiff-Legged Deadlifts	Kicking Snap-Back Muscles
Curls	Pulling and Uppercut Muscles
Forearm Curls	Grabbing Muscles
Abdominal Crunches	Strong Abs Benefit All Techniques

There are many specific weight training routines to develop the muscles for speed. For the sake of conserving space, I will just show you my routine. Adopt it, discard it, or use it as a foundation to branch off on your own.

I have been lifting weights since Charles Atlas ruled the beach; in fact, I even entered a physique contest several years ago (yes, I had to shave all the hair off my body). Anyway, now that I no longer care about looking pretty, my primary interest is in building greater speed and power for the martial arts.

As of this writing, I have been using the following routine or a variation of it for about six months. Even in that short period, I have already noticed considerable improvement in certain karate and grappling techniques.

Chest

I begin my routine with three to four sets on the pec deck machine, which does a good job of approximating the movement of a sweep block. I put on enough weight so I have to really squeeze the last 8 to 10 reps.

My second chest exercise is flat or inclined bench dumbbell flies. This movement approximates the back-fist when the dumbbells are lowered; when raised they develop the sweep block motion and, to some extent, the roundhouse punch. I do two to four sets of 8 to 10 reps, and use maximum exertion on the last two or three reps.

My last chest exercise is actually a combination chest, back, shoulder, and triceps exercise, but I include it with my chest training because my pecs are already trashed from the other two exercises, and this pushes them to exhaustion. It also brings into play the exact muscles used in straight punching. In fact, I call it cable punching (clever, huh?).

But before I describe the cable punch in more detail, a word on reps is in order. I learned the following method of doing repetitions from reading several articles about a real powerhouse named Rich Barathy. I don't know where he is now, but back in the 1980s he appeared on several talk shows demonstrating his dynamic and powerful breaking abilities. He attributed much of his strength to his method of weight training.

Barathy didn't just isolate each muscle group, such as the triceps, biceps, and lats, he broke each group down into two or three sections, like the upper triceps, middle triceps, and lower triceps. Not only did this approach leave no part of the muscle untouched, but he felt it also created a link between his muscles and his mind. It allowed his mind to "trigger" each muscle section, which gave him greater control over the flow of energy through the muscles used in a specific strike.

Cable punching strengthens the exact muscles used in the reverse punch. Even if you normally don't begin your punch at your side, do it in this exercise so that you work the full range of the movement.

Start with your punch chambered and punch halfway out for 10 reps. Begin the second set at the halfway point and punch out to the extended position for 10 reps.

Finish a third set of 10 reps, punching from the chambered position to the extended position.

Using this idea with cable punching is easy. I grasp a cable handle and turn my back to the pulley machine. I assume my punching stance, hand chambered, hips rotated away from the front. I push my punch to the halfway point just as my hips begin to rotate, and my opposite hand retracts halfway. I do one set, 10 reps with each hand.

On the next set I double the weight and begin the punch where I left off at the halfway position. I make sure I finish my hip rotation and retract my opposite hand all the way. I then return to the halfway point and punch out again. I do one set, 10 reps.

On the third set I do the complete punch. I sometimes use the doubled weight, or I may drop back to the weight I used in the first partial rep set. Sometimes I triple it. Again I do one set, 10 reps.

In just a few weeks, cable punching has improved my reverse punch and jab, and that includes my left arm, which has a permanent, debilitating injury.

Back

I only recommend bent-over rowing exercises to guys I don't like. This is where you bend over and pull a barbell to your chest, then lower it to the floor. I've seen too many people hurt with this move, though some are able to do it for years without injury. It's dangerous because you probably don't know if you are susceptible to it until a low-back vertebra goes "boing," punches through your flesh, and flies across the room.

Pulldowns are safer. Sit on a bench under a lat machine, grab the bar (there are a variety of bars to choose from), pull it down to your chest, and then slowly let it up until your arms are extended. This is great for developing the specific muscles used in punching and retracting and the muscles used in grappling, such as when you pull your opponent toward you. Do four sets, 10 to 12 reps.

Shoulders

Because of old injuries, I do mostly dumbbell lateral raises for my shoulders as opposed to overhead pressing. Laterals will develop strength for general pushing and will add some strength to outside blocking and backfisting. With bent arms, raise the dumbbells up at your sides, turning your fists so that you are leading somewhat with your little fingers as if pouring water out of your thumbs. Do four sets, 10 to 12 reps.

Biceps

An exercise called 21 will tax the dickens out of your biceps as it works them in sections. Do seven half-reps with either dumbbells or a barbell, curling from the fully extended position at the bottom until your forearms are horizontal with the floor. Then without stopping, do seven reps from the halfway point all the way to the top. The final seven reps begin at the bottom and curl all the way to the top and back down again. All three sections count as one set. Rest a minute and then do one final set of 21 reps.

These curls develop the muscles involved in uppercuts, those used to retract most hand strikes, and those used in all grabbing and pulling techniques.

Triceps

My triceps are worked quite a bit in the cable punching exercise, so I usually limit my triceps exercises to two that will develop my backfist strike.

In the first exercise, I use the cable pulley system because I can easily emulate the backfist movement with it. I begin in the on-guard position, the cable handle in my lead hand. I extend my hand out as if doing a backfist, returning it only halfway, since returning it too far can strain the tendons around the elbow joint. As I extend my arm, I rotate my fist just enough to strike with my two large knuckles. Do three sets, 8 to 10 reps with each arm.

This exercise works all the muscles used in the backfist. Start in the chambered position and slowly extend your arm. Hold the extended position for a couple of seconds to strengthen the muscles around the elbow. Do three sets of 10 reps.

This is a variation of the last exercise. If the dumbbell is heavy, don't lower it further than is pictured because you may strain the tendons in your elbow.

Extend the dumbbell straight up, aiming with your two large knuckles. Do three sets of 8 to 10 reps.

The next backfist exercise is a variation of the last one. For variety, I do each for a month at a time.

I lie on my right side, holding a dumbbell in my left hand, my arm bent so my forearm is about horizontal with the floor. I extend it straight up as if I were doing a backfist, again aiming with my two large knuckles. I return it about halfway and then extend it again. If you lower it further than horizontal, you risk straining your elbow joint. I do three sets, 8 to 10 reps with each arm.

Legs

If you like squats, do them. I don't, so I don't. It can be argued that they are valuable in the grappling arts, especially for wrestling and judo. As with bent-over rowing, there is an inherent risk to your lower back with squats, not to mention they will give you a butt the size of a dump truck.

As far as I'm concerned, the risk is just too great, so I go with leg extensions, which I think are more practical for the kicking arts anyway. According to a physical therapist I know, it's less stressful on the knee joint, tendons, and ligaments to begin the movement extended 45 degrees, rather than vertically as most machines position you. From the 45-degree angle, extend your legs to full contraction, holding that position for three to five seconds to develop the supportive muscles around the knee cap. Do one set with your toes pointed straight up, one with your feet angled outward, and one set angled inward. The three angles help develop all the kicking muscles of the thigh. Do three to five sets, 10 to 12 reps.

Leg curls are important exercises, though often neglected by weight trainers. They develop the muscles that retract your leg after you kick and the ones directly involved in the hook kick. For complete well-rounded development, angle your feet in each set as you did with the extensions. Do three sets, 10 to 12 reps.

Forearms

Strong forearms also mean strong wrists and hands, all of which are important in the fighting arts.

I begin with a grip exerciser and squeeze away for about three sets of 15 reps. I then go right to the dumbbells, placing my forearms on my thighs so my hands are extended out past my knees. I do three sets with palms up and three sets with palms down, 15 reps each. I finish with the air-grabbing exercises described later in the grappling section. I do them as fast as I can for about 30 seconds each. The idea is to force the tough forearm muscles to contract as fast as they can after I have taxed them with the weights. This gives the forearms one hellacious pump.

I hate forearm exercises because they hurt so much, but in the few months since I've been doing this routine, I have noticed a big difference in my grip strength as well as my grabbing speed.

Abdominals

You will be able to twist, turn, bob, and weave with greater speed if you are not cursed with the "dunlop" disease—that condition where your belly has "done lopped" over your belt. The abdominal muscles are involved in every martial art move you make, and, when in condition, they add explosive speed to your punches, kicks, and grappling techniques.

I'm a firm believer in hard abdominal work, and we do 12 different crunch exercises in our school, too many to illustrate here. We do 200 to 300 reps per workout, having found that it's better to do a dozen different crunches 20 times than one crunch exercise 250 times.

There is nothing special about the crunches we do. If you don't already know a few, you can find them in just about any bodybuilding magazine, so-called women's magazines, and on all aerobic exercise tapes.

I do this entire 30- to 40-minute workout twice a week. I have found it productive, and I will continue to experiment with innovative ways to make it better. You should do the same.

Muscle Balance

It's important in your weight training to always work toward balanced development. Without balance great speed will never be possible.

A prime example of poorly balanced development can be found among weight trainers who favor the bench press. This is common among young lifters, usually teenagers, whose muscles respond quickly to the exercise. When they see the fast results, they hit the bench even harder, neglecting other muscles, especially their backs. As one teen asked me, "Why work my back? It's behind me."

Bench presses use the muscles of the shoulder, pectorals, triceps, and, to a lesser extent, the back. But the back muscles are very much involved in punching. The lat muscles under the arm help drive the punch forward, and the muscles around the shoulder blades and spine assist to pull the arm back. To punch at your maximum speed, a well-developed chest must be balanced by a well-developed back.

Most kicks use the muscles on the front of the thighs to thrust the kick outward, and most kicks require strong hamstring muscles, those located on the back of the thigh, to bring the foot back. Yet all too many martial artists work only the front of their thighs, grunting out reps of heavy squats, while failing to do anything for the backs of their legs. Know this: if your leg development is not balanced, you cannot develop optimal kicking speed.

Go through your exercise routine to ensure that it is well balanced. Are you hitting the muscles on the back of your arms as hard as you do the showier ones on the front? Are you working the muscles on the side of the neck as hard as you do those on the front and back? If you do a lot of crunches, what are you doing for the sides of the waist?

Think of your body as a complete unit or, better yet, as a long, powerful section of chain. If there is one weak link, the entire chain is weak.

Train for balance, eliminate the weak links, and enjoy the rewards of greater speed.

The
Quickness Diet

"Never eat more than you can carry."
—Miss Piggy

C an you eat yourself fast?

Well, that might be overstating it a little, but what can be said without exaggerating is that you can definitely eat yourself slow. For sure, soda pop, Twinkies, donuts, and Big Macs are not going to do a thing to help you develop speed and, over time, will do much to slow you down and tear you down.

Stating it simplistically, slim and trim is faster than roly-poly. Granted there are some fat martial artists who are fast, but they would be even faster if they had less weight to move. Martial arts instructor Glen Smits summed it up this way: "The less body fat on and in between the muscle fibers, the greater the potential for efficient muscular activity."

Besides obesity, there is the issue of general health. There is a reason you feel trashed when your hard workout is over, why you feel a general weakness, localized muscle tremors, and a desire to just nod off in the old easy chair. When you train hard for speed, you are stressing your reflexes, muscles, joints, tendons, cardiovascular system, and heart. After just a few minutes of hard training, you are beginning to drain your body of vital energy-giving, growth-giving, indeed, life-giving nutrients. After an hour they are drastically depleted, and your body is crying out to have them replenished. Your ol' bod has treated you good; now it wants something back.

But what do too many martial artists do after their hard workout? They eat and drink crap. They stop at the local Dairy Burger and grab a 97-ounce cola (the cup is so large it has a pounding surf), a 99-percent-fat gut-bomb burger, and a large order of double-dipped-in-lard fries.

Their bodies are already struggling to recuperate from the workout, now they have to struggle to assimilate two pounds of impossible-to-digest garbage. Their internal system is either going to give up on the digestive process or give up on recuperating from the workout; at the most, it will do only a little of each. You might be able to get away with this for a short while. Though your body is amazingly tolerant, it's still keeping tally of these abuses. It will pay you back at first by making you feel sluggish, slowing your progress, and teasing you with minor strains and pulls. It does this as a warning that you are not replenishing what you have torn down. But if you are like many people, you will ignore these signs and keep right on expecting quality out as you put garbage in.

I use to work out in a gym where a big-name National Basketball Association (NBA) player lifted weights. For three years he was plagued with injured knees, twisted ankles, strained elbows, and a myriad of other owies that gave him more time on the bench than under the net. One day the gym owner took him aside and talked to him about his eating, which was a poorly constructed vegetarian diet and who knows how much junk food.

The NBA star allowed the gym owner to design a diet for him, still vegetarian but better designed so the assort-

ed legumes, grains, fruits, and vegetables all comple-
mented each other. In short order, the NBA player discovered that his improved way of eating gave him more
energy and supplied all the valuable nutrients he needed
to replenish his body after a hard-fought game. He was
injury-free that year, and his team went on to win the
NBA Championship.

One out of 10,000 people can get away with eating a
lousy diet their entire lives. They are the ones who live to
be 100, enjoying cigarettes and bourbon right up to the
end. Most people, however, self-destruct and die on such
a regimen. The problem is this: you don't know if you are
the one out of 10,000 until you get a birthday cake with
100 candles on it. On the other hand, if your final cake
had only 52 candles, you know you were not one of them.

But we are not talking about longevity here, though
it's a nice side benefit of being selective about what you
put into that big hole in your face. We are talking about
fueling your body properly so you can enjoy your martial
arts training, make progress in general, and—the big
issue as far as we are concerned now—develop awesome
speed. Some top athletes fuel their bodies with junk—
some even brag about it during interviews—but imagine
what they could do if they consumed a healthy diet.

Now that I have convinced you about the logic of
proper fueling for health, recuperation, and speed development, let's look at some general information about
what you should be putting into your body. We are not
going to discuss the many eating fads around, such as
munching on your lawn clippings or making soup out of
your cat's fur balls (why is it all the bizarre diets come
out of California?). For sure, there are as many strange
diets around as there are strange Californians, er, people
advocating them.

Most nutritionists agree that the best way to eat for
superior athletic performance is also the best way to eat
for general health. For example, lowering your fat intake
lowers your cholesterol and triglycerides, reducing the
possibility of having a stroke or heart attack. Cutting

back on red meat minimizes toxic by-products and reduces digestive problems. Increasing your intake of high-fiber complex carbohydrates provides you with double the health benefits.

Let's look a little closer at protein, carbohydrates, and fats, as well as vitamins and minerals, to see how they relate to your development of speed.

PROTEIN

Have you noticed that the same people who advocate megagrams of protein are the same people who market it? There have been articles written by bodybuilding champions—who just happen to be writing for bodybuilding magazines that manufacture protein supplements—who claim they consume two or three grams of protein per pound of body weight. That would be 450 to 675 grams of protein for a 225-pound lifter. The truth is, if a bodybuilder really consumed that many grams of protein for any length of time, his kidneys would go off like a whoopee cushion under a fat lady's butt.

Excess protein is not good for you. You don't need it, it won't make your muscles bigger, and it won't make you punch and kick faster. It also takes about eight times as much water to burn a calorie of protein as it does one from a fat or carbohydrate. This is an important consideration when you are already losing water through heavy perspiration from your hard workouts.

Years ago, doctors, nutritionists, and athletes assumed because our muscles are protein, an increase in protein consumption would mean an increase in muscle size. We now believe this is false. Your body can only handle so much per day—about one-half gram per pound of body weight. A rule of thumb is that only 10 percent of your total calorie intake should be protein, even if you are weight training and practicing martial arts. I know of one top bodybuilding champion who made gains on only 40 grams of protein a day.

The truth is this: as a hard training martial artist you need just a little extra protein to rebuild what you tear down during your workouts. Make sure you get it everyday, but don't go overboard.

FATS

The whole issue of fats can get quite complicated, but for our purposes here, we don't need to delve too deeply into the issue.

An excessively high-fat intake can affect your training and your speed. Excess fat will bind with red blood cells, causing them to clump within arteries, slowing blood circulation and, in time, decreasing the volume of oxygen carried to your muscles. If you consistently consume more fat than carbohydrates, you will begin to drag because you won't be able to replenish the glycogen stores from your last workout. This will snowball, and, in short order, your workouts and your progress will suffer.

Before a workout, it is especially important to avoid a high quantity of fats, such as consuming a burger, milk shake, and fries. This places too heavy a burden on your digestive track, taking blood away from your muscles.

A rule of thumb is to keep your fat intake down to around 10 to 15 percent of your daily caloric intake.

CARBOHYDRATES

Carbohydrates are a great source of fuel because they are made of carbon, hydrogen, and oxygen molecules. They should make up about 70 percent of your caloric intake. But be careful which kind you eat.

There are two kinds of carbohydrates, simple and complex. Simple carbs are sugars, the kind found in candy and some fruits. They are called simple because their chemical structure is made up of only two molecules hooked together, making them highly digestible and quickly absorbed into the blood stream. Simple carbs—that chocolate bar you ate before your workout—

will give you a quick shot of energy, but it will only last about 10 minutes. If you are like a lot of people, you will come down from the rush to a lower energy level than before you ate the candy.

Complex carbohydrates consist of long strings of molecules, which are not as quickly digested or dispersed into the bloodstream. This is a good thing, because when the process is slower there is not a dramatic rise and fall of your blood sugar, so the energy-producing effects last longer. Complex carbs are found in foods such as pasta, breads, potatoes, corn, and cereal.

MARTIAL ARTS SEMINAR DIET

Maintaining energy is a concern if you are at an energy-draining, all-day seminar. Some martial artists like to sneak a piece of baked potato or a wedge of orange during breaks. Others, who are not affected by the pronounced ups and downs of simple sugars, like to eat a hunk of chocolate every 40 minutes or so (I'm one of those). You will have to experiment to see what works best for you.

PREWORKOUT DIET

Keep it simple and keep it light. The majority of your calories should be complex carbs. OK, you can have a few simple carbs as long as you combine them with the complex ones, but the complex ones must make up the majority. This will keep your energy level constant to better get you through your two-hour workout.

PRE-COMPETITION DIET

Your diet should not fluctuate to any great degree throughout the year. If you maintain a low-fat, moderate-protein, and high-carbohydrate diet all the time, you should not have to change it when you are in competitions. If you are unable to train for awhile, you may want to reduce your caloric intake some; or if you are going to train harder than usual for a week or compete on Saturday, you might want to increase your carbohydrates a little. Other than that, you will feel best and train at your optimum if you maintain a consistent, healthy diet.

Make proteins, fats, and carbohydrates important to you. They are the important fuel that supplies the necessary energy to get you through your speed training and the building blocks to repair your tired and torn-down tissue after your workout.

VITAMINS AND MINERALS

It's not necessary for our purposes to make a list of all the known vitamins and minerals and what they do for you; that information can be easily found in many other places if you want to research further. You should know, however, that vitamins A, D, E, and K are fat-soluble and are stored in your body. Since an excess of these may have a toxic effect, it's a good idea to stay within the recommended daily allowances (RDA) for them. All other vitamins, however, are water soluble, and any excess will be excreted in your urine.

There is controversy in some circles as to whether you should take vitamin/mineral supplements. Some people swear by them; others say they are unnecessary. I've never thought there was a controversy; I've always taken them, especially high doses of vitamin C and the Bs. I've never gone along with the argument that I get all I need in my diet. The reality is that I don't always eat well, and even when I eat healthy food, I don't always know how many vitamins and minerals I'm getting. So I supplement to make doubly sure.

Vitamins and minerals will not give you immediate energy, but a lack of your daily requirement over time will begin to take its toll on your energy level, as well as on your soft tissue and bones.

So what is your daily requirement? Who knows? That too is controversial, with many athletes arguing that the Food and Drug Administration's (FDA) recommended daily allowance is too low. Below, I have listed the RDA of vitamins and minerals for triathletes. Though these people train harder than most of us do, I think the listed quantities apply to hard-training martial artists. I have followed a similar vitamin-mineral supplementation for years, and I know of others who do the same. I feel good about the benefits I have gotten from my supplements and plan to continue them.

Try the following plan or experiment to see what works best for you.

TRIATHELETE'S RDA

Vitamin A	5,000 IU
Vitamin B Complex	20–50 mgs (I take 75 mgs)
Vitamin C	200–400 mgs (I take 2,000–5,000 mgs)
Vitamin D	400 IU
Vitamin E	30–60 IU
Iron	20–30 mgs (more for menstruating women)
Calcium	200–600 mgs (more for women)
Magnesium	350 mgs
Potassium	200–400 mgs
Phosphorus	600–1,000 mgs
Zinc	10–30 mgs
Iodine	100 mgs

CAN COFFEE HELP YOUR SPEED?

Maybe, but you need to decide whether it's worth it. In a study at Ball University, several athletes drank coffee without knowing it (don't ask me how they managed that), and every one of them found that their performance improved considerably; in particular, they were able to exercise for 7 percent longer than without coffee. I have more endurance when I drink two cups of coffee before a martial arts workout, and I am able to lift weights more intensely on a blast of coffee.

So what is the bad news? For one, caffeine makes your blood sugar level fluctuate. It also contains lots of acid that can cause heartburn during your training, and it's a diuretic that will send you trotting to the john more than once during your class. All these can have a negative effect on your workouts. Some people experience all of the effects, while others won't at all. I have never had any of these problems, but I drink only one cup before karate class.

Though one cup doesn't render quite the desired effect, drinking three cups can be detrimental. Studies have shown two cups of coffee to be the optimum. Also take into consideration that espresso is stronger than supermarket coffee.

It takes 15 to 20 minutes for the coffee to get into your system and about 45 minutes for the total effect to hit. In other words, drink it about an hour before you train.

Will hot java make you faster? The jury is still out on that. But it will let you train a little harder and a little longer toward your optimal speed.

Perception and Reflex Speed

I'm going to start with perception and reflex speed because that is where your offensive and defensive speed begins. If you don't perceive it—see, hear, or feel it—there is nothing to reflexively respond to. Putting it differently, if you don't perceive someone standing behind you with a 2 x 4, you are not going to be able to defend against it.

For our purposes here, we are going to combine the actions of perception and reflex. Therefore, the majority of the drills and exercises in this section will train them simultaneously. First up are training methods designed to help you develop fast reflexes to visual stimuli.

DRILLS AND EXERCISES TO DEVELOP FAST VISUAL PERCEPTION

Gazing

Before we begin to look at all the drills requiring a response to visual stimuli, let's examine where you should look when facing your sparring partner, tournament opponent, or a street fighter.

Sifu Dan Anderson demonstrates that when you watch your opponent's eyes, you will not see or react to an attack until it is halfway to you, too late to block it.

During my first couple of years as a young-buck *karate-ka*, I never looked directly at my sparring partner, but would focus my eyes 12 to 15 inches to either side of him. I did this for two reasons: I was young and trying to be different, and I had convinced myself I could better detect my opponent's movements by not looking directly at him. And I could, as long as his skill was no higher than white or yellow belt. But as I went up in rank and my partners progressed too, looking off to the side no longer worked.

But if you watch the hands, you will see the initial move and be more likely to block the attack.

"Where do you look?" is probably the most commonly asked question by beginning martial art students and occasionally some advanced ones who are still unclear about what works best. Should you look at your opponent's hands, feet, eyes, elbows, chest, or hair? The answer is like so many others in the fighting arts: there is no absolute answer.

Sifu Dan Anderson of Dan Anderson Karate in Gresham, Oregon, is a tournament fighter who has won so many trophies that if they were melted down they could supply the raw material to build a hundred Oldsmobiles. He teaches that if you look at your opponent's eyes and shoulders you will miss the agents that can hit you: the hands and feet. By watching the agents, Anderson says, you can detect the instant they begin to attack and can therefore determine their direction. This allows you to intercept them more quickly, thus minimizing the element of surprise to you.

Instructor Robert Peter, a student-instructor of Shidare Yanagi Aiki Jujitsu and author of *The Black Belt Manager: Strategies for Creativity, Power, and Control*, advises watching the attacker's elbows and knees, as opposed to his hands and feet. Because there is less motion with these swivel joints, it's easier to detect the faster fist and foot.

Many other instructors believe that to be reflexively fast, you should never look directly at your opponent's weapons but rather develop the skill of not looking at anything. The great sword fighter Musashi referred to this learned skill as gazing at the opponent rather than looking at him. The idea is to take in all of him, maintaining an unobstructed mind so you can react to whatever comes your way. If you focus on your opponent's notoriously fast backfist, he just might kick you in the groin. "If you look at the sword, you will be killed by the sword," goes an ancient saying. In other words, if you focus on one thing, it disrupts the natural calmness of your mind and inhibits your ability to perceive.

Try the following experiment. Understanding that your opponent can't move without first moving his upper torso, you gaze at his sternum rather than his hands and feet. Gaze as if you were looking through his chest, as if he were not there and you were looking off in the distance. From this center point, notice how you are able to see his hands and feet without moving your eyes (in a moment we will look at some drills you can do to develop your ability to increase your peripheral vision). When your focus is not stopped, meaning your attention is not pinpointed on one thing but is open and flowing, you will

Gaze at your opponent's chest and see whether you can detect when he is going to punch or kick.

bring all of your opponent into your vision, rather than just his feet and hands.

Actually, this approach is indirectly in agreement with what Dan Anderson and Robert Peter teach. By gazing at the center and maintaining a calm mind, you are able to see your opponent's hands, feet, elbows, and knees in your peripheral.

You will have to experiment to see what works best for you. You may decide on the method favored by Dan Anderson or Robert Peter, or you may find that looking at your opponent's center mass works best for you. You may even find that doing a little of each is the way to go.

If you find you are getting hit consistently and you can't determine any other cause, examine how and where you are looking at your opponent.

Developing Peripheral Vision

One major contributing factor to fast reflexes is a fine-tuned sense of awareness. Through the practice of the assorted reflex drills illustrated in this text, you will develop fast and explosive responses to attacks and openings. But in order to respond you must be aware. That is, you must first be able to see the stimulus.

As we said earlier, perception is just the first part of your reflexive response. After perceiving the stimulus, you must select a response and put it into action.

But before you can react at your greatest speed in all three of these phases, you must *relax*. I've mentioned this before, and I will mention it several more times in this text: you can't react physically if your mind is cluttered with fear, anxiety, and anticipation. For you to be at your most responsive, your mind must be as calm as the surface of a still lake.

The second requirement for increasing reflex speed is the development of your peripheral vision. It's important to have the ability to see wide when dealing with multiple attackers coming at you from all directions. Without it, you may find yourself focusing on one attacker while a second and third hit you from the sides.

It's also needed when facing one opponent. If you focus your attention too closely on one thing, say your opponent's feet, he just might punch you in the head. But if you direct your gaze at his upper chest area, basically his center mass, you will be able to see his feet and his hands in your peripheral vision.

While some people are born with good peripheral vision, others have to work to improve theirs. The good news is that it isn't hard to develop. Try the following drills and *see* what happens.

Drill 1

Here is a simple exercise you can do right in your easy chair. Look across the room and find something to focus on, such as a spot on the wall, a nail, or a smear on the window. Look at it but concentrate on seeing everything around it, as far to the right, left, up, and down as you are able.

When you have developed the ability to see as far as 10 o'clock to your left and 2 o'clock to your right, it's time to practice "speed seeing." This time begin by looking away and then quickly back to the focus point, striving to see as much as you can in your peripheral vision as fast as you can.

Drill 2

In this drill you will work your peripheral vision by using mobile targets. Begin by facing a training partner directly to your front at 12 o'clock, while a second partner stands off to your left at 11 o'clock, and a third positions himself to your right at 1 o'clock. Your gaze should hit your 12 o'clock partner about chest level, though you are striving to see his hands and feet with some clarity and as much as you can of your training partners.

If you can't see the side partners at first, have them step a little closer toward 12 o'clock until you can see them better. Now, look at your center partner for a minute or two and concentrate on seeing his hands and feet with greater and greater clarity. At the same time, push to see as much of your side partners as possible.

When your peripheral vision improves—improvement may happen immediately or may take several weeks—the side partners should move a few inches farther to your sides and continue to do so as your ability to see them increases. "See them" means you can see a fuzzy image at the edges of your peripheral vision, but, though it is fuzzy, you can detect movement.

Your objective is to be able to see your side partners even when they are spread out as far as 3 and 9 o'clock. When you have progressed to this point, your partners should make some kind of movement: twisting their feet, fiddling with their belts, nodding their heads. Can you detect what these movements are? If not, keep working until you can. We are not talking about ultraclarity here, but you need to see well enough to know what the movement is.

The last phase of this drill is to have your side partners throw kicks and punches at you. Don't bother with blocking or reacting in any other way to the attacks. The purpose of the exercise is to increase your awareness and the width of your peripheral vision, and to educate your eyes to recognize punches and kicks thrown from the far edges of your sight.

Drill 3

This visual reaction drill helps develop your eye and muscle coordination and increases your ability to observe with your peripheral vision.

Assume your fighting stance and face a training partner who has one hand against his chest and is holding a hand-held punching pad with his other at a height you can jab. Your direct gaze should be on the pad, not on the hand on his chest, though you can see it in your peripheral vision.

Your partner creates a visual stimulus by lifting his index finger, leaving the rest of his fingers flat against his chest. When you see the movement in your peripheral vision, reflexively snap out your lead jab and strike the bag. At first he should lift his finger boldly, but as your

Assume a fighting stance and face your partner, who is holding a striking pad in one hand and holding his other hand against his chest. To benefit from the exercise, it's important to look directly at the pad, but see his other hand in your peripheral. The instant his finger flicks out, explode with a backfist.

skill increases, he should make the movement more subtle, thus forcing you to concentrate intensely. It's important that you concentrate on the pad and not look directly at your partner's hand, though you can see his hand well enough to detect movement. Stay relaxed and loose and then explode on the visual stimulus.

If you find you are watching his hand instead of the pad after several minutes of fast punching, you are probably getting tired—it's time to quit. You are not going to help your speed by continuing after you are fatigued. About 10 to 15 minutes is the maximum.

Drill 4

This is another fun exercise to sharpen your observation skills and reflexes.

Begin by facing straight ahead to 12 o'clock as your training partner assumes a position about 45 degrees off to your left at 10 or 11 o'clock, or to your right at 1 or 2 o'clock. As you gaze toward 12 o'clock, use your peripheral vision to observe your partner toss a rubber ball to you. Your objective is to catch it without diverting your eyes toward it.

If at first you need to take a quick look toward the ball, go ahead. But since your objective is to be able to see it by using only your peripheral vision, look directly at it less and less as you progress. As you improve, your partner should inch further to the side, toward 3 or 9 o'clock, depending on which side he is on. When you start to show improvement again, he should throw the ball progressively faster.

Drill 5

Face your partner, who is holding a kicking shield in front of him. Focus your gaze on its center but see his feet in your peripheral vision. Your objective is to respond reflexively with a roundhouse kick into the bag when he wiggles his toe.

A good way to warm up your reflexes and kick your fastest is to practice your first few reps close enough

Stare straight ahead to 12 o'clock as your partner at 2 o'clock tosses a ball at you. Use your peripheral vision to help you make the catch.

that you only have to lift your leg and kick. Once you are comfortable with that, back up to a range where you must shuffle step or scoot in to kick the bag. This will benefit you in three ways: first, it will develop your peripheral vision; second, it will help you develop a fast reflexive kick; third, it will force you to work on speed stepping, an area often neglected by many martial artists.

Drill 6

The concept in this peripheral observation drill is similar to that of Drill 5, except that the emphasis is on developing whiplike speed, good control, and the ability to snap the leg back rapidly.

You and your partner assume fighting stances and face each other close enough for you to kick his leg without taking a step forward. Your partner does not hold a bag this time, but rather stands motionless and lets you kick at him. Gaze at his upper chest and expand your sight to his feet. When he lifts his big toe, you reflexively pop a controlled lead-leg roundhouse kick at his calf and then snap it back instantly. Repeat 10 times with each leg.

Next, move back from your partner so that you have to shuffle step or scoot forward to kick at his leg. Do 10 reps on each side.

Once you begin to feel good about your improved speed in this drill—it may take several days or even several weeks before you see marked improvement—progressively raise the height of your kicks so that you are kicking at his thigh, groin, and abdomen.

When you develop your peripheral vision to where you can detect the subtle movement of your partner's toe, imagine how easily you will see a chambered leg or an incoming leg sweep.

Consider all of these peripheral vision drills as basic foundation exercises that should be practiced often. As with weight lifting, kata practice, and judo randori, you must continue to train in order to maintain your skill level. The beauty of these drills is that by improving your awareness, they indirectly develop your reflexes, speed, control, and power.

And remember, to respond at your quickest, *stay relaxed.*

LIGHTS ON/LIGHTS OFF DRILL

Though the visual stimulus in this drill is more glaring than a side kick in your face, it will sharpen your reflexes. The only equipment needed is a totally dark room and a flashlight with a button that can be poked to flash the light on and off.

This drill can be conducted with one student or as many as 50; it really doesn't matter. If there is usually a radio on during the class, shut it off so the only stimuli are visual.

The students line up and assume their fighting stances, and the lights are shut off. They are given a moment to adjust to the darkness before the instructor pokes the flashlight button for no longer than a quarter of a second. When the button is released, the room is once again dark. The students' objective is to react to the light with a designated technique, such as a backfist or a front kick.

The instructor usually begins the drill from the front of the class but can wander around the room after a few repetitions. Because the room is dark, the class is unable to see where he is, so when the light suddenly flashes from the side or behind, the students must turn and respond with their technique.

It's a fun drill that creates a sense of edginess because you don't know when the light is going to flash or from which direction. The light creates a startle reflex, and if you are relaxed and ready, it will spark an instantaneous response.

Snappy techniques such as the backfist, side kick, front snap kick, and lead jab work best for quick, reflex responses. That doesn't mean you can't practice with other less snappy moves, such as high hook kicks or front thrust kicks. In fact, once you catch on to it, you can respond with elbows, knees, or even combinations.

As is the case in all speed drills, you need to remain relaxed. To respond at your fastest, you must keep your mind clear and not try to anticipate where the light is going to flash. If you anticipate and you are wrong, you must shift mental gears to react, thus defeating, not to mention slowing, your reflexive response.

Lights on/lights off is an excellent drill to increase visual reaction time and the explosiveness of your response. It's fun to do, and you may want to do it in high repetitions. That's OK, but as in all speed drills, remember not to push it past your fatigue point.

PLAY BALL DRILLS

The kid in you will like these exercises. You don't need a mitt, but you do need some balls.

Drill 1

Stand a couple of feet away from a blank wall and face your training partner, who is armed with a half-dozen tennis balls. As he lobs them at you one at a time, your job is to evade, block, or hit them. If you have a third person to act as a chaser to get the balls, the drill will be more continuous.

At first you can restrict your responses to just evasive movements. Then after five minutes, change your response to blocks, and after five more minutes switch to punches or kicks. After you have become comfortable with all three types of responses, you can react in whatever way your reflexes dictate.

To increase the intensity of the drill, your training partner can throw the balls progressively faster and at different heights, such as to the head, chest, groin, and legs.

You start out with large balls, such as soccer balls, and then reduce the size to that of tennis balls (golf balls hurt like the dickens).

A variation is to have two partners throw balls at you.

When your partner throws a ball at you, you can block, evade, or punch it.

They must not overwhelm you, but throw enough of them and with enough velocity to give you a good workout.

Drill 2

This is a takeoff on the first drill, but a variation more applicable to the grappling arts. You will need a sponge ball, one about as large as a soccer ball.

Stand with your back to a wall and face your training partner, who is armed with several balls. For the sake of this drill, imagine an invisible vertical line dividing your upper body in half. Your partner should throw the ball slightly to the outside of the invisible line so you have to twist your body to avoid being hit. If the ball's trajectory is toward your right side, you should twist to the right; if it's thrown at your left side, twist to your left. As you twist, reach out quickly and grab the sponge ball as if you were grabbing an opponent's attacking limb.

When the ball is thrown at your abdomen, imagine that you are being grabbed around the waist. A toss to your chest simulates a push or punch to that target; whereas a ball thrown face high would act as a high punch. At each trajectory, twist away and grab the ball before it passes. Some students even pantomime executing a partial grappling technique geared to the height of the attack. Your partner should throw the ball faster and faster as you improve.

A good follow-up to this drill is to have your partner thrust his hand toward you at the same three levels he threw the ball. Your response is to twist in whichever direction is applicable, grab the attacking arm, and apply a grappling technique.

Drill 3

This is another reflex drill that will keep you on your toes as you develop fast hand-to-eye coordination. You need a blank wall, a few tennis balls, and a couple of partners, one to throw balls and another to chase them.

Standing about five feet away from a blank wall, face it and assume a fighting stance. As your partner stands behind you and slowly lobs a ball over your shoulder at the wall, your objective is to catch it as it bounces back toward you. You won't see the ball until it hits the wall, or maybe just an instant before. To test you at a variety of angles, your partner should lob the ball over each shoulder and over your head.

As your reflexes develop, and it won't take long, take one step closer to your partner. After another five to 10 tosses, take another step closer and continue advancing on the wall until you are about two feet away. The final stage is to have your thrower toss the balls faster and faster. When you get to the point where you can't catch any of them, you know you have gone as far as you can.

Drill 4

This drill is a good device to break the ice with a new class or to stir up some enthusiasm in an old one. The side benefit is that it will sharpen everyone's reflex speed and get them to use their peripheral vision. You will need a space large enough to make a circle 20 feet in diameter and a dozen or more hand pads, arnis sticks, tennis balls, and anything else that can be easily thrown but won't cause injury if a student fails to make a catch.

Make a circle of about 15 to 20 people. Begin the exercise by tossing a hand pad around the circle. As soon as one person catches it, he tosses it to someone else in the circle. After a couple of minutes, add a second pad to the toss and a minute or two later add a ball and then a shoe. Continue adding items until there are 6 to 10 objects flying around the room.

The object of this drill is to catch the items and get rid of them quickly before another object arrives. Getting whacked in the side of the head is the best incentive to think and react quickly. Make a fun rule that when someone misses a catch, he has to drop to the floor and do five push-ups.

The last stage is to use only arnis sticks. This is more dangerous, so you should slow it down at first and use no more than four to six sticks. For safety, the sticks should be thrown vertically or horizontally, never end over end or like a spear.

Use your creativity to make this drill effective. For example, throw the ball up with your left hand and catch it with your right. Or throw it with one hand and clap both hands before you catch it.

Drill 5

In this hand-to-eye coordination and reflex drill, you need two balls, a tennis ball and one about the size of a soccer ball.

Lie on your back, legs stretched out, ball in your hand. Lob it straight up and then catch it with one hand as it comes down. Don't try to get too precise in how you throw the ball because you don't want it to always go straight up and come straight down. The more off course the throw, the quicker your hands have to be to snatch it out of the air. You can throw it up with your left and catch it with your right, or throw it with your right and catch it with your right. Vary your responses and make the drill more interesting and beneficial.

To develop speed in arnis, toss a ball about head high and then strike as many times as you can before it hits the ground.

Try it with the big ball and then the small one. Get creative and try to make it more and more complicated. For example, clap your hands three times before you catch it or wait until the very last instant to move so that you to have snap your hand out to get it.

The first time I did this exercise I forgot my ball-loving dog was in the room. It ruins your concentration to have four paws and a hairy belly land on your face.

Drill 6

Try this drill with punches or arnis stick strikes. Toss one or two tennis balls in the air and execute as many strikes as you can before the balls hit the ground. You are not trying to hit them, but throw as many air punches as you can before they land. Good arnis fighters can deliver 10 strikes before the balls land.

Drill 7

This is primarily an arnis drill, but you can modify it and use karate punches.

You can use tennis balls, though arnis fighters use marbles. Choose three to five balls or marbles, each of a different color. Mentally, assign a different technique to each color; for example, red gets a horizontal strike, blue gets a diagonal strike, and so on. Now, hold them behind your leg so you can't see them. Throw one at a time up in the air and deliver the strike you have assigned that color. Stay relaxed, keep your mind clear, and strike out with speed and accuracy.

When using karate techniques in the drill, use colored tennis balls and find someone willing to chase them for you. Assign each a different technique and strike as described with the marbles.

BAG REFLEX DRILLS

Double-End Bag

Be cautious in using the double-end bag because until you get the hang of it; you can easily overextend your elbows when trying to connect with its irregular swing pattern. But once the bag is learned, it's a great device on which to develop quick reflexes and hands.

When hitting the bag for the first time, most students hit too hard. That is not the objective with the double-end bag. Hit it lightly at first to establish a rhythm and then every so often smack it a little harder to send it out extra fast. This means the bag is going to also come back extra fast, so be ready to block it, check it, or punch it

The double-end bag is great for developing reflexes and speed.

again. If you don't react with one of these options quick-ly, chances are you are going to get bopped in the head.

To send the bag straight out and back, you must hit it straight on. If you hit it a little off center, it will go out at an angle and come back at a different angle, forcing you to change your position to hit it in the center again.

Chances are you won't hit it in the center, so you will launch it on yet another angle. You have to have quick footwork and hands to keep up with this goofy bag.

It's just a matter of experimenting to learn what all you can do with this exercise. For example, you can back-fist and then reverse punch; jab and then elbow; reverse punch, headbutt, and then backfist; or jab, duck, and then jab again.

It doesn't take long to develop skill on the double-end bag. By the second or third workout, you will be smacking it around like a pro and be on your way to faster reflexes, hands, and footwork.

Two-Pad Surprise Drill

This drill is designed to sharpen your reflexes when responding to two bags presented in such a way as to create an element of surprise. Depending on the position of the bags, you will be forced to make a quick decision about which target to strike first and which technique to use.

Assume your fighting stance and face your partners, who are standing in front of you at about 11 and 1 o'clock. Each partner is continually moving a hand-held striking pad, making its height and angle fluctuate.

Your objective is to strike the targets when the moment is right and with as much speed as you can. The drill is not to hit one bag one time and then the other bag the next time. Instead, hit one and then immediately hit the other. You decide when to hit and which technique best applies to that situation.

To move at your greatest speed, you can't take the time to consciously think about what you are going to do; by the time you have decided, the bag positions will have changed. You must strive to keep your mind calm and clear so you can react subconsciously at your fastest reflex speed.

When you train repetitiously with reaction drills, you will condition your subconscious mind to react instantaneously to an attack or an opening. When you have reached this level of expertise, your reactions will be explosive when compared to your snail-like, conscious-mind reactions.

A word about your training environment. Though you might get into a real fight in a noisy, rowdy setting, your training place should be quiet. Because you are working on conditioning your subconscious, you will improve much faster without distractions. Shut off the music and eliminate as much noise and confusion in your training space as you are able.

ARNIS ATTACK DRILL

This is a good drill for arnis, although you can easily do it with punches and kicks. It's a visual drill that will teach you to become alert in the initial stage of your opponent's attack.

You and your partner face each other, standing at a distance where you both can extend your sticks at arm's length and touch the ends. Assume your fighting stances and take a moment to mentally and physically relax, especially your weapon arm.

The moment your partner begins a move, you strike with your stick at whatever opening is available. When his shoulder dips, foot scoots, or eyebrows arch, you respond with a single blow or multiple hits. Don't step across the gap to get him. Strike at the available target as if you were already close enough to hit it. Your objective here is to develop quick target recognition at a safe distance.

Practice the drill with your sticks in various positions. One time start with your stick cocked at your shoulder, another time with the stick held low. Your partner can vary his stick positions as well. This will give you a variety of visual stimuli and targets.

If you notice your partner telegraphing, say so. Help one another so that you both benefit from the drill.

CIRCLE OF DEATH

In spite of the name, this drill is fun and will help you develop fast reflexes as you respond to attacks coming at you from all directions. It's versatile, so you can use karate kicks and punches, grappling techniques, or weapons such as arnis sticks or knives. You need 6 to 10 people to make it beneficial.

Let's say you are in the hot seat, meaning you are in the circle as a half dozen or more "attackers" surround you, far enough back so they have to take a step to close the gap. All attackers get numbers and then change places so that they are out of sequential order.

The instructor assigns the techniques to be used in the drill. When he calls out a number, the attacker with that number steps in and attacks, to which you respond with a block and counter. Because the numbers are out of sequence, you don't know if they are coming from the front, side, or rear. This adds an element of surprise, thus forcing you to react reflexively.

If you are a white belt in karate, the attackers should use simple techniques—for example, only roundhouse kicks. If you are a black belt, the attackers can hit you with anything. You can restrict the drill to just blocking, or you can block and counter.

Keep this thought in mind as you strive for fast blocks: to block quickly, you must perceive the attacking agent within the first three to five inches of its takeoff. Your block will be fast and effective if you can intercept the attack at about its halfway point. But if you don't perceive it until halfway, you probably won't be able to react quickly enough to block it. Therefore, not only is perceiving the attack important, but recognition of type and angle of attack is necessary to respond with speed. We will illustrate several drills later to help in this recognition. As you get proficient with the exercise, the instructor calls out a number, waits a second, and then calls out another so that two attacks come almost on top of each other. As you

When your opponent dips his shoulder to punch, react instantly with your closest weapon.

progress, the instructor calls out two or three numbers at the same time.

The instructor needs to monitor the drill to ensure that it doesn't turn into a melee. Because the center person is getting attacked from all sides, anticipation and anxiety often turn the drill into a spontaneous sparring match. This isn't what it's about.

The circle of death works well with arnis sticks. Again, if you are new at arnis, the attacks and responses should be simple. If you are advanced, increase the difficulty level and the speed of the attacks.

Use grappling responses with the same format as described, except your response will be jujitsu, aikido, or some other form of grappling technique. Depending on your skill, you can make the drill as simple or as involved as you want.

When you have been attacked by each person once or twice, you will assume number one's place in the circle, and he will take yours in the middle. The circle can remain static during the drill, or it can slowly rotate around the center person so that he can't figure out which number belongs to which person. If at any time the center person looks as if he knows the attackers' numbers, simply renumber everyone. Remember, the drill is to enhance reflex and response speed, so the element of surprise needs to be kept fresh.

You can modify the circle of death to make it as easy or complex as you like. As your skill improves, the attacks and the responses should become more complex and intense. In the process your reflexes and speed will increase accordingly.

FRRRRREEZE DRILL

My students love this drill because it's fun and fast and they can see benefits from it almost immediately. It's also a versatile exercise you can use to increase your reflex speed in many areas of the fighting arts. It requires three people: two fighters and one person to act as a trainer.

To illustrate, let's say you and your partner want to work on increasing the explosive speed of your reverse punch. You will be called "A" and your partner will be "B." Face each other in your fighting stances and begin moving around as if you were sparring. Don't punch or kick; just circle and move back and forth as you flow from one stance to another.

When the trainer calls out "freeze," you both stop, holding whatever positions you happen to be in, no matter how silly or awkward. Then the trainer calls out a letter, say A, who instantly punches B in whatever frozen opening is available.

The fighter whose letter is called must recognize an opening and nail it as quickly as possible. When the moment is frozen, the opening is easy to see. By hitting it quickly, the fighter is learning to respond reflexively to an opening.

At first, the fighter who remains frozen should hold his position until his partner hits his exposed target. Once both fighters are responding quickly and with confidence, the freeze time should be reduced to one second. Now when the trainer calls "freeze" and then "A," A must respond within one second or B will begin moving again and dissolve the opening. Often, dramatic improvement can be seen in just one workout, but usually it takes three or four sessions.

You can also practice the drill using kicks. This is harder because you are going to have to kick fast to get them in, but then speed is what the drill is all about.

If you are having trouble getting your punch or kick in to the opening fast enough, practice at close range. When you are in the moving-around phase, stay close enough to each other so that when the order to freeze is called, you can hit without having to take a step to close the distance. Remember, when you are close to a target to begin with, your strike will land sooner, as if it was thrown faster. But as you adapt to the drill, move around at the normal sparring interval from each other and practice closing the gap with fast footwork and a punch or kick.

Use the freeze drill to practice foot sweeps. After both fighters are told to freeze, the fighter whose letter is called must quickly determine which of his opponent's legs can be swept, based on proximity and weight distribution. Decrease the freeze time as you progress.

Use the drill for grappling practice. When your letter is called, instantly apply the best grappling technique based on your opponent's position. You need to recognize

In the freeze drill, you and your partner stalk each other without throwing techniques. When the instructor calls out "freeze," you both stop instantly.

his weakness, decide which technique is the most applicable, and then move in and apply it. Practice until you can move instantly and explosively.

The freeze drill is a fun way to sharpen your ability to instantly recognize an offensive opportunity and then physically react to it.

The instructor then calls out "A" or "B," and that person explodes into the closest open target.

THE HANGING PAPER DRILL

Hang an 8 1/2 x 11 sheet of typing paper from the ceiling by two lengths of thread or string. As you move around the paper, hit it with a jab or reverse punch. After the first hit, the paper will twist and turn in an irregular pattern. Your objective is to strike the paper

As the paper moves about in the wind, wait until you can see the X and snap out a punch before the exposed letter disappears.

every time a flat side is presented to you. To develop accuracy, draw a small X in the center and on each side and aim for it. If you want a challenge, place a small, rotating fan at a distance so that it blows the paper a little each time it passes.

Your objective is not to tear the paper down, but to react to the target as quickly as you can. This will help develop speed, accuracy, and timing.

There are other visual drills throughout the book, but they have been placed in other sections. Reflex response to touch will be covered in the grappling section.

AUDIO REFLEX DRILLS

Although there are few situations in sport or street fighting where you would respond to an audio stimulus, it's used in these exercises to fine-tune your reflexes and get you to respond explosively. The bottom line is this: whatever you can get to sharpen your reflexes and make you go off like a bomb will be of benefit in other areas where explosive reflexes are important. If you want to practice both the audio and visual drills on the same day, practice one for a few minutes and then the other for a few minutes, for a combined total of 15 to 20 minutes. Practice until you are tired and then quit. Remember, you can't progress when you are fatigued.

Snapping Finger Drill 1
Begin by facing your partner, who is holding a hand pad high enough so that you can hit it with a jab or backfist. His other hand is held behind his back so that you can't react to any premovement he might make with his hand when he snaps his fingers. When you hear the sound, you reflexively strike the bag. Stay relaxed, don't anticipate, and let the sound ignite you just as a fuse ignites an explosive.

Snapping Finger Drill 2
In this drill, you punch at two training partners holding pads, who are positioned at 1 and 11 o'clock. Assume your fighting stance and hold your gaze at 12 o'clock, though you can detect the pads on both sides. One of your partners holds his empty hand behind his back and snaps his fingers. Your objective is to respond with two fast punches, one to each pad.

This takes considerably more effort than the first finger-snapping drill. If the bag holders are standing close together, punch one bag and then turn at your waist and hit the other. But if your holders are spread six feet apart, you will have to switch stances in between the strikes. It doesn't matter how you do it as long as you do it reflexively when you hear the finger snap.

Clapping Stick Drill

This audio-response drill can be done by the entire class. The instructor assigns every person a technique, has the students take their fighting stances, and then moves to the rear of the class. At his whim the instructor strikes two sticks together to make a sharp report. Upon hearing the sound, the class responds with the technique, not toward the instructor but toward the front of the room.

When I do this drill, I like to wander around the back of the room so that the students hear the sound coming from different locations. They still respond to the front, but their ears have to be sharp to hear the stimulus.

The instructor should clap the sticks in broken intervals, so that there is not a pattern established. He claps, waits five seconds, claps, waits 10 seconds, claps, waits two seconds. The intervals must be irregular to make the drill a true reflex response exercise.

Sometimes the instructor strikes the sticks together twice, in which case the class responds with two fast techniques. Two or maybe three techniques are about maximum for an audio reflex response. Any more and the element of surprise is no longer present.

One variation is to practice the drill in total darkness. With the lights on, the class members assume their fighting stance and face the front. After the lights go out, the instructor slaps the sticks together, and the students respond with a punch, kick, or whatever technique has been designated. After a few repetitions, the instructor reduces the sound level to a tapping sound, forcing the class to strain to hear. He can also wander around the room, slapping the sticks together in various locations.

Barking Drill

The instructor uses his voice in this drill, but differently than simply counting out reps as the students punch and kick. The purpose here is to ignite a reflex action to the sound.

The way in which the instructor uses his voice is all important. The command should be a sharp bark, as opposed to the relatively longer enunciation required to say a number. The best utterance is the old Marine Corps bark "hup." It's emitted in a burst of air from deep down in the belly and, when done correctly, isn't much different from the clap of two sticks together.

Audio Bag Drills

With these drills you will use an audio stimulus to spark your response to hit a punching bag. These drills will help you in three ways. The audio stimulus will sharpen your reflexes, striking a bag will develop your power, and by pushing your punching and kicking speed you will become faster.

Drill 1

This drill requires two people to hold the bags for you. Begin by assuming a ready position with your back to the bag holders, who are standing to your left and right, each with a hand-held punching pad held at face height. When one of the holders calls out "hup," you turn and reflexively strike both bags.

Your objective is to react instantly to the audio command, striking the closer bag first, as if an attacker is moving toward you, and then move quickly to strike the second bag. You want your movements to be economical, fast, and optimal, given your position relative to the targets. Check yourself to ensure that this is being done and listen to feedback from your pad holders.

The positions of the bag holders should change slightly with each repetition to keep the reflex element fresh. For example, one holder can move back a step, and the second holder forward a step. Or one person can raise his

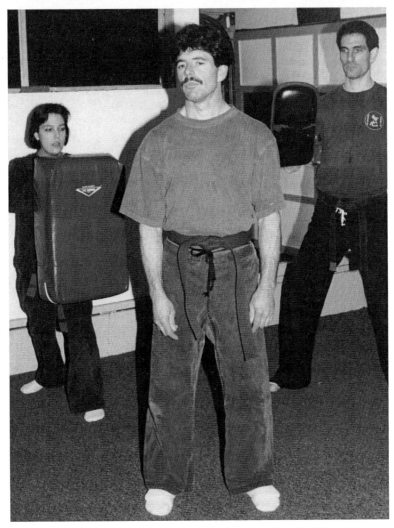

In this audio drill, stand with your back to two bag holders.

pad, and the other can lower his slightly. The idea is to present a fresh picture each time you turn.

Drill 2

This variation begins the same as the first drill did, but here your training partners are holding kicking

On the command of "hup," turn and kick the shield if it's closer and then strike the hand pad.

shields. On the audio command, you turn and respond to the closer "threat" with an appropriate kick and then immediately kick the second shield.

Your response needs to be reflexive and delivered as fast as you can, using your best form and the best kicking technique for the situation. Your holders should vary the positions of the bags a little for each repetition.

Drill 3

This drill is set up the same as the other two, except

If the hand pad is closer, hit it first and then kick the shield.

that one holder has a kicking shield and the other one has a pad for a hand strike. You respond with a kick to the shield and a hand strike to the pad. Again, the holders should change the picture with each repetition.

Drill 4

This should be used after the first three drills to see whether you are moving fast enough.

On the "hup" command, turn and respond to the striking pads as before. But this time the closer holder silently counts, "One thousand one," and then jerks the pad away. The most distant holder counts, "One thousand one, one thousand two," and jerks the pad. If you have not struck by the end of the count, you have lost the opportunity.

After the target has been pulled away two or three times, your embarrassment will make you analyze what you are doing wrong. It's probably one or more of the following reasons:

- Your perception of the targets may be too slow.
- This drill may be too advanced for you.
- You may be thinking too much and not reacting reflexively.
- You may have excessive movement, which uses up your time.
- Your transition from pad to pad may be awkward and slow.
- Your techniques may not be the best choice for the targets.

Drill 4 requires very fast reflexes and movement speed. If you are having problems, it may be because you have not achieved the necessary skill level required of the drill. If you are not ready for this phase, swallow your pride and return to the first three drills until you have sufficiently sharpened your reflexes and increased your movement speed. Then try it again.

CHAPTER 5

Developing
Movement Speed

In the last section, you looked at exercises and drills to increase your reflexive response to visual and audio stimuli. Now you will examine exercises to push you to punch, kick, grab, block, step, duck, bob, and weave faster and faster. Though some of these exercises overlap to some extent into perception and reflex responses, they are not the primary objective here. This section looks at ways to help you increase basic movement speed independent of outside stimuli.

Let's begin this section with a drill that has been one of my favorites for a long time. I can get worked up into such a psychic lather with this one, I sometimes scare myself.

RED-LINE DRILL

I learned this drill at a Chuck Norris seminar back in the 1970s. I have used it for years in my training, and I like to use it to push students to reach further and further toward their maximum speed. It's an exhausting drill, aerobic, calorie intensive, and one that is as much a mental effort as a physical one.

The red-line drill forces you to dig deep into yourself to pull out whatever it takes to move faster than you ever have before. There is no restraint in the red-line phase. There is no "I'll hold back a little and do it harder next time." To reap maximum benefit, you must seize the moment and pull out all the internal strength you have to push yourself to reach speeds greater than you thought were your maximum.

Don't use new techniques in the red-line drill. New moves need to be polished so that all the bugs are out before you push for speed. Red line should use techniques you can do easily and flawlessly.

Let's look at the four phases of the red-line drill using a lead-hand rising block and reverse-punch combination.

Phase One

If you have practiced the rising block-reverse punch combination a million times before and you are thoroughly warmed up, you can skip this phase and begin with phase two. Phase one is primarily used when you want to combine two or three techniques you have previously practiced only singularly, not in combinations. Or this phase can be used to polish combinations you have not worked on for a while.

Phase one is a time to ensure that you are blending moves properly. Check to see that your blocking hand is snapping up and then retracting as you step forward and punch. Then check to see that you are retracting the punch as you step back to your on-guard position.

All of this is done slowly so you can check for errors and eliminate them before you move on to the next faster phase. Do 10 or more repetitions on each side.

Phase Two

In this phase, the combination is performed at medium speed to establish a good mind-body connection and to get a sense of how it feels doing it at a greater speed than in phase one. Do the complete movement: block, step forward, and punch. Make an effort to use proper form, keeping the muscles relaxed until impact, and to breathe out sharply at full extension of the punch.

Do no fewer than 10 repetitions on both sides, more if you feel the need. *Do not move on to phase three if there are any rough spots in the combination.* Because the next phase is to block and punch fast, you don't want to entrench an incorrect movement in your subconscious mind.

Phase Three

In this phase you block and punch as fast as you can. Don't hold back just because you know you have another phase to do. Psych yourself into a combat mind-set. Snap the blocking arm as if you are really trying to avoid getting struck, thrust your foot forward to cross the gap, and nail your invisible opponent in the gut with a fast punch.

In this phase "fast" is what you can achieve while still managing to maintain proper form. Slam out 10 repetitions on each side and then take a 60-second breather as you mentally prepare for the next phase.

Phase Four

Now it gets really interesting. In this phase you push yourself beyond what you previously thought was your top speed. Up till now, the speed you used in phase three was what you have accepted as your fastest. Wrongo. You have a little more in you, but you have to reach down to pull it out. It's there, but to bring it out you have to believe it's there.

Accept the fact that in this phase your form is going to go down the toilet. Don't worry about it; it's OK. Your only interest at this time is speed, pushing yourself to go faster than what you thought was your fastest in phase three.

Begin by relaxing. *Only relaxed muscles can move fast.* Reach down inside yourself and pull out that hate, rage, hurt, or whatever is within that inflames your killer instinct and pushes your speed faster than ever before.

Your breathing is faster now; your eyes are glazed over, maybe even watering a little. You are getting seriously wired.

If the emotions are not happening naturally, fake them. Force your breathing to quicken, as if you are enraged and psyched, and glare hard at the invisible target in front of you. Fake it hard enough and it will start to really happen.

Begin with the block, snapping it up faster than ever before. If it went too high or covered your face, that's OK. Now lunge forward with your lead foot. Maybe you went too far to the side, or your stance was too narrow. That's OK. Now, explode that punch. You probably lost your balance a little, rotated your hand too late, or retracted your opposite hand improperly. That's OK.

Do 10 repetitions on both sides, a few more if you are having a good time and are really into it. Then stop and catch your breath. You went faster than in phase three, didn't you? Sure, your form was off, but you will get that back in a minute. What is most significant is that you pushed beyond what you thought was your top speed. What was your ceiling is now just a little higher. It wasn't just a physical effort, but you had to mentally reach into those dark places we all have and pull out whatever it took to push you to a higher level.

Feel good about what you just did.

Back to Phase Three Again

Remember, your form went into the toilet in phase four, so now you have to get it back since you never end a training session with improper form in your mind. In phase three you still had good form, so you need to go back and do 10 more phase-three fast reps to conclude the drill by executing the techniques the way they are supposed to be executed.

If you are in shape and still have plenty of energy left, you just might notice a slight increase in your speed the second time you go through phase three. If not, don't fret. It will just take a few more sessions with the red-line drill before you see improvement.

Practicing Long Combinations
One Technique at a Time

You can also practice long combinations in red line, such as a sweep block, same-hand backfist, reverse punch, and lead-leg roundhouse kick. One way is to progressively add techniques to your combination, practicing each new phase at phase-three speed. It works in the following way.

Assume your fighting stance, left leg forward, and relax your body, especially your arms. Execute a fast, face-high sweep block. Do a total of 10 reps; then change stances and do another 10 with the other hand.

When you finish, shake your arms loose and get ready to add the second technique, which is a backfist with the same hand you blocked with. Do 10 reps of the sweep block-backfist combination on each side at fast speed. Don't hold back because there is more to do. Go as fast as you can while maintaining good form.

Add the reverse punch next and do 10 reps of the now triple-move combination on each side. Your final stage adds the roundhouse kick, during which you maintain good form while moving as fast as you can. By the time you finish you will have performed 40 reps with the sweep block, 30 backfists, 20 reverse punches, but only 10 roundhouse kicks. Therefore, the next time you train you should begin with the roundhouse kick, first doing 10 reps on each side; then add the reverse punch and do 10 reverse punch-roundhouse kick combinations. Do 10 more with the backfist added, and last do 10 with the sweep block. You are not doing them backwards, just combining them in reverse order to get a balanced workout.

Building a combination in this fashion allows you to put all of your energy and concentration into each technique, adding the next one only when you feel ready. If you are ready after 10 reps, great. If it takes you 25 reps, that's OK too.

Once you are executing the combination smoothly, you are ready to advance to phase-four speed red line, where you will do the four techniques all together and

faster than you ever have before. When you have completed 10 on each side, which were a little sloppy but faster
than you did them earlier, rest for a few seconds and do 10
more at phase-three speed to regain your good form.

Here is an interesting way to "think" your combination faster. Instructor Robert Pater suggests that you not
think of a four-count combination as four *individual*
techniques. Pater advises, "Visualize complex moves as
one large movement without steps or edges. It's critical
to think 'one' rather than 'one, two, three, four.'"

Free tip: Hitting in combination should not just be an
exercise, but rather a way you normally think about hitting. As a police officer, I have seen bad guys take a powerful hit from a police baton and not blink an eye. I once
hit a guy in the ribs with the side-handled baton about as
hard as I've ever hit anyone. He was a leader at an anar-
chist street demonstration and had been warned to cease
and disperse, but he was psyched and determined not to
give up his right to break windows and start fires. Now, I
never liked the side-handled baton, but I got pretty good
with it because I had to teach it so much in the acade-
mies. I mention this only to point out that I could deliver
a pretty strong blow with it. So I delivered one, putting
all 215 pounds of me into the whipping motion, hitting
the scumbag dead center in the ribs and raising a small
cloud of dust off his filthy clothes. I stood back to let him
fall, but instead he just turned away from me and started
yelling orders to the other demonstrators.

That did two things. It hurt my feelings and made me
remember what I already knew but had let slip from my
mind because I thought I possessed such awesome hitting power: in real fighting, you must hit more than once.

Make combination hitting part of your style or philos-
ophy, and practice it in the red-line drill so you can deliver those blows like a blur.

Multiple Same-Kick Drill

In this red-line drill, you execute the same kick five
times, beginning at medium speed, progressing to fast,

then red line, and back to fast speed again. The first five reps are to mentally get into the movement, the second five to execute the kick as fast as you can, the third set of five to push yourself faster than ever before, and the last five to get back any form you lost during red line.

Assume a fighting stance and begin with a lead-leg hook kick. You can step forward with it or remain in place; it's your choice. Pop the hook kick out, snap it back, and set your foot down. Do five kicks with each leg, rest a minute, and then kick five more times at the next speed. Continue in this fashion all the way through the speed levels.

Use this drill for as many different kicks as you can but don't continue past your fatigue point.

Kata Practice

I believe that one of the "secrets" to improving kata is training sequentially, practicing only two to four moves at a time. This allows you to concentrate all your energy into one small section of the kata.

Since this drill is to build speed, choose a kata with which you are familiar so that you don't have to spend time correcting improper techniques. Begin with the first two to four movements and progress through the kata, doing only two to four moves each time. Do the sequence first at medium speed, then fast, then red line, and then return to fast speed again. If your kata has a hundred moves, you better have an ambulance stand by.

I have trained this way in kata for years and have yet to find anything that beats the results I get from it.

Speed Drills and Fatigue

Pushing your speed can be quite taxing, especially when working on combinations. You will defeat your own purpose if you train when you are tired and when your muscles have not had sufficient time to fully recuperate. Therefore, don't practice the red-line drill more than twice a week; in fact, once a week is preferable.

*Practicing speed reps is
one of the best ways to
develop movement speed.
However, it's critical to
know when to stop
because the onset of
fatigue will start to bring
out such small errors as
dropping the rear hand
at the conclusion of the
hook kick.*

Actually this suggestion applies to all speed drills, but let's make sure there is no confusion about this. I warn you throughout this book not to continue speed training when you are tired. To develop speed, your muscles and brain must be rested, recuperated, and raring to go. When I tell you to stop the drill when you are tired, I am referring only to the speed drill you are working on, not necessarily your training session.

In my school, we practice speed drills at the beginning of the class after the warm-up. Then after 20 minutes or so, we stop the speed exercises and go on to grappling, using weapons, and sparring. Speed drills are only practiced when you are fresh.

SHADOWSPARRING

Shadowsparring is an excellent tool to develop quickness in your movements and smoothness in your stance changes as you move around, bobbing and weaving, punching and kicking. Because there is no opponent to block your techniques, disrupt your footwork, or throw techniques back, everything you do will be complete and unchecked. There is no set pattern in shadowsparring; you can move however you want and throw whatever you want. It's your fight; keep it simple or make it fancy.

Though most of the shadowsparring drills listed here are to develop movement speed, there are just a few (all of which are clearly labeled) that depend on visual and audio stimuli to spark your quick response. But for the sake of continuity, I have kept all of the shadowsparring drills together.

Watch Yourself

Try shadowsparring in front of a large mirror so that you can observe your movements and make corrections. If you have a tendency to hold your hands too low, the mirror will reflect it. If you have a habit of pulling at your pant leg, the mirror will show you. And if you are ugly, the mirror will tell you that too.

Watching yourself in the mirror is a good way to check your form before you start pushing your speed. When you begin, move around at medium speed and correct any problems you see. Once you feel good about how you look, pour it on.

Do It to Music

Shadowsparring to music helps develop timing and makes the exercise fun and somewhat painless, even when pushing speed to the max. Find music that you like and that has a pronounced beat, and then crank it up as loud as you want. As you shadowspar, move to the music's rhythm, and when you hear the pronounced beat, explode with your technique. You don't have to throw a technique on every beat, but when you do, it should be on the pronounced note. This will establish a nice flow to your movements that eventually will overlap to sparring with a live opponent. Additionally, the music will cloak your fatigue, allowing you to exercise longer.

Shadowspar Like Bruce Did

Bruce Lee used shadowsparring to develop quickness in all his movements. Sometimes he did it just in the air, while other training sessions he would dance around a heavy bag, moving and hitting with quick, sharp techniques.

Shadowsparring with Weights

Shadowsparring while holding one- or two-pound weights in each hand or with one- or two-pound weights strapped to your ankles will help build endurance, strength, and ultimately speed in the specific technique being worked.

A major concern of shadowsparring with weights is the risk of injury to your joints, especially if you lock out your punches and kicks. Even without weights it's never a good idea to lock out your joints when you punch or kick. Be aware of your joints so that you will still be

Shadowsparring at medium speed with two- to five-pound dumbbells will develop strength and speed in the very muscles used in sparring. Never, never lock your elbows out.

training years from now. Always shadowspar with weights at medium speed and never use full extension.

A nice benefit of throwing techniques with weights attached to your limbs is that the added weight gives you a feel for which muscles are brought into play and a greater awareness of the specific body mechanics involved.

Practicing arnis techniques at medium speed with baseball bats will develop strength and speed. Be careful not to snap your wrists because the excessive weight may cause injury.

Shadowsparring with Heavy to Light Arnis Sticks

This is an idea I got from instructor Rick McElroy of McElroy's Martial Arts Academy in Hilton Head, South Carolina. He teaches to first train with heavy weapons and then progressively decrease the weight until you are using a very light weapon. This not only gives you a sense of increased speed, but your muscles will grow stronger from the added resistance, which results in increased speed.

McElroy suggests that for arnis training you begin working with a heavy pipe or a baseball bat; reduce the weight by going to the heavy, thicker type of arnis sticks; and finally decrease to the half-inch lightweight arnis sticks.

There are several ways you can incorporate this into your shadowsparring. One is to shadowspar at medium speed for five one-minute rounds with a metal pipe or baseball bat, resting a minute between rounds. Repeat this two to three times a week for a month. The next month shadowspar with heavy arnis sticks, increasing the number of one-minute rounds to eight. On the third month, you decrease to the lightweight sticks and shadowspar for however many rounds you want.

Another training approach, the most popular one, is to go through all three weights in one workout, say two two-minute rounds at each weight level. The heavyweight and medium-weight weapons develop strength, while the third set with the lightweight weapons develops speed in the fast-twitch muscles.

Don't try to flip the heavy weights around as you would a normal arnis stick. You may be able to lift the weight easily, but rotating your hand, whipping your wrist, and abruptly stopping the weight in the air will injure your forearm muscles and tendons.

Shadow sparring with heavy weapons should be done at the end of your regular arnis training session or used as supplemental training on solo training days at home.

Shadowsparring with the Class

Shadowsparring is a great solo workout when you can't make it to class or when you want to have a sparring session where you can work on pushing your speed without interference from a partner. But it can also be practiced in a class setting, so you can use other students to liven up your training while still sparring alone.

Though I've added my own modifications, I got the idea for the following drills from an article by Manuel Siverio called "Shadow Sparring" in the October 1986 issue of *Blackbelt* magazine.

Drill 1

With this drill, the instructor holds a couple of sticks and stands behind the class as the students spar with their invisible opponents. The students have been instructed that when they hear the crack of the stick, they are to respond with a designated kick, punch, or some kind of combination.

The sound sparks a reaction as if responding reflexively to a sudden opening in an opponent's defense. If the student's designated technique is a block and counter, the sound represents an opponent's attack. If the designated technique is a kick, the sound represents an opening.

This will help you identify slow places in your response, which are commonly a result of muscle tension or excessive expectation.

Drill 2

This variation on the audio drill starts the same as the first audio exercise except this time the instructor smacks the sticks one time for a single response, twice for a double response, and so on. Of course, you can get creative with this variation and make it so that one smack of the sticks designates a kick response, two means a punch, and three means a combination. Or one hit means turn left and attack, two hits means turn right and attack, and three means turn all the way around and attack. Use your imagination and make it work for you.

Drill 3

This version is fun and adds a bit of competition to shadowsparring. Pair up, maintaining about six feet of distance from each other so that there is never contact, and then begin shadowsparring. When the instructor claps his sticks, respond freely or with a designated technique. The objective is to move faster than your opponent.

The following drill, drill four uses a visual stimulus to spark a response.

Drill 4

In this drill, the instructor will kneel either in front of the class as the students shadowspar or in the center of the room as the students form a large circle around him and shadowspar. Whichever way it's set up, the students keep an eye on the instructor as he holds a stick or a glove about three feet off the floor. At his discretion he drops the object. The students' objective is to respond with a technique before it hits the floor.

The drop signals a sudden opening, and the time it takes the object to hit the ground represents the amount of time the target is exposed. If the students don't react in time, the object hits the ground, and the opportunity is lost.

These shadowsparring drills can be used for karate, arnis, knife training, and grappling. Use your imagination and create your own variations. When sparring with an imaginary opponent, you can apply your full concentration to your techniques without concern for being blocked or attacked. As such, you can focus your attention on maintaining relaxed muscles and delivering fast kicks and punches.

Use the beat of the music or your instructor's voice to spark a reflex response, or just explode on your own. Put all you have into your fight, striking out as fast as you can and retracting even faster.

PARTIAL REPS

Partial reps is an exercise I made up several years ago, or at least I thought I had until I saw a similar version in a karate magazine a while back in which jeet kune do instructor Paul Vulnak was demonstrating it as a good way to increase speed. And Vulnak is an instructor to listen to. Although I have never met him, I have seen a couple of his videos and find his speed to be extraordinary.

As the name implies, practicing partial reps means you are doing only part of a complete repetition. By doing only, say, one-third or one-half of the rep at a time, you can concentrate on putting more energy into a smaller portion of the movement. Here is how it works.

Backfist

Assume your fighting stance and relax your muscles, especially your lead hand, arm, and shoulder. When you are ready, launch a backfist, stopping halfway out. There is no snap back because you are not throwing a complete repetition. Put everything you have into it, mentally, physically, and emotionally—in other words, explode. Do 10 reps on each side.

The second phase is to complete the backfist motion, beginning where you stopped and then snapping it all the way out. Again, you put everything you have into the motion; do it hard, do it fast—explode. Do 10 reps with each arm.

Backfist and Lunge

First practice the partial backfist motion in the first drill, which doesn't involve your lower body; when you feel comfortable with that, you are ready to coordinate your footwork with your arm movement.

When you execute the first half of the backfist, lunge out with your front foot, but only halfway. Work to increase the speed of your footwork just as you push to increase the speed of your fist. After you have finished a set of 10 reps with the first half of the movement, do a set of 10 with the last half, stepping all the way out as quickly as you are able.

It's amazing how soon you can develop a fast backfist with this drill. But you have to be aware of tensing your muscles. It's easy to tense up when you move only a little and put maximum energy into an explosive burst. If that happens, just drop your arms and shake them as you relax mentally and physically.

You should do another 10 repetitions of the backfist and lunge in its entirety so that you don't end the drill with partial movements remaining in your head.

Reverse Punch

When practicing the exercise using the reverse punch, launch the punch from where your fist is normally held. This position may be the side of the rib cage, the center of the chest, or from an on-guard position next to the jaw.

Launch the punch halfway out or to the point where your fist just begins to rotate and your hips begin to turn. You can incorporate a partial forward step if you want, or you can work just your arms first and then do an extra set incorporating your footwork. Once again, the idea is to explode fast, driving your fist partially out, twisting your hips partially, and retracting your other hand partially. Do 10 reps on each side.

Begin the second phase of the drill with your fist halfway out. Punch the rest of the way as fast as you can, twisting your hips and pulling your other hand all the way back. If you are incorporating footwork, complete your forward lunge in this phase. Do 10 reps on each side.

Do another set of 10 reps, executing the complete punching motion.

Partials are also an effective way to practice your kicking techniques.

Front Kick

A partial movement with the front kick involves lifting your knee into the chambered position as fast as you can and raising it as high as you normally do when you throw a front kick. Stay relaxed, do 10 reps on each side, and strive to kick faster and faster.

To perform the second half of the kick, assume the chambered position. Because you are beginning at the halfway point, you won't have the momentum to drive the kick forward as you would if you were doing the entire movement. To kick with speed, you will have to use just the muscles of your legs, hips, and abdomen. As always, relax first, explode your foot forward, and snap it right back. Remember, the snap back is all important in delivering a fast kick. Kick out at 100 mph and return it at 175 mph. Do 10 reps on both sides.

Virtually all kicking movements can be broken down into partials reps. Determine the chambered position for the kick and practice just a portion of it as fast as you can. Then practice the second half. As with the hand techniques, you should always do a final set of the entire kicking movement.

Partial Footwork

Use partials to work on your footwork. So often, students work only on the speed of their hand and foot techniques, forgetting that if they can't close the gap fast enough to get to their opponent, fast punches and kicks won't matter. Isolating just the footwork without adding any other techniques will allow you to concentrate only on enhancing your speed.

Assume your fighting stance, left leg forward. Move your right foot up to your left, shifting your weight to your right leg as if you were going to kick with your front. Resume your fighting stance and repeat the step again and again and again. Each time you execute the move, push to move faster and faster.

Lunging with the front leg requires greater concentration than stepping up with the rear foot. You must coordinate driving off the back leg while thrusting the front leg forward and then scooting the rear leg up. What makes the move partial is that you only lunge a couple of inches, as opposed to 12 to 36 inches, which is usually the case. Because it's a relatively complex movement, be cautious that you don't tense your legs and hips as you force speed. Mentally relax your lower body and imagine your legs weighing only ounces.

How To Benefit from Watching Partial Reps

Here is a way of doing partial reps with a partner that will benefit both of you.

Face each other and assume your fighting stances. Now, as he throws out the first half of the backfist, you simply maintain your fighting stance and watch him. Your objective is to look for all the subtle and not so subtle movements involved in his technique. As his hand snaps halfway out, look for a muscle tensing in his neck, a slight dipping of his shoulder, a subtle turning of his waist, and the tell-tale trajectory of his forearm.

The more you watch, the more your subconscious brain absorbs all the nuances a person uses when throwing a technique. Later, you will recognize these signals when you are sparring or fighting. For example, when your opponent begins to launch a backfist, your brain, having been educated from the drill, will recognize the early stages of the attack and alert you to block or counter quickly.

You can practice this two-person version with all of your partial-rep exercises. It's a great way to kill two birds with one stone, so to speak. One person benefits physically from the speed drill while the other develops his powers of observation and educates his subconscious mind.

Raw Limb

Another version of a partial drill with the reverse punch is to execute only the arm movement without turning the waist, rotating the pelvis, extending the shoulder, or stepping forward. I call the movement "raw limb" because you use only the speed of the isolated arm.

Assume a natural stance, feet parallel and shoulder-width apart. Chamber your fists at your sides and relax your body, especially your right shoulder and punching arm. Now, keeping your left fist chambered at your side, punch straight out with your right, making sure not to flip your elbow to the side as so many people carelessly do. Punch out and snap it back in one quick movement.

Feels weird, doesn't it? That is because your arm is doing the punch without any help from the rest of your body. Only your arm is involved, just the raw limb. Do 9 more; then do 10 with your other arm, always pushing to go faster and faster.

Two people can benefit from the partial-rep drill. Here the female student watches the body mechanics as the male executes the first few inches of a reverse punch and just the chambering portion of a front kick.

Raw-Limb Kicking

This kicking drill comes under the heading of raw limb because you use only the leg muscles, leaving the waist, hips, and momentum uninvolved.

Begin by standing naturally, arms at your side, feet parallel with each other. Relax mentally and physically. Now, throw out a side kick to the left with your left leg, turning your right foot as much as you normally would and leaning in the opposite direction as much as you normally would. Snap your foot back to your knee and set it on the floor. Do the same thing with your right foot, then again with your left, and so on.

Front kicks are executed by simply lifting your knee, kicking forward, and returning your foot on the same path all the way to the floor. Use the same stance for the back kick, kicking at least belt-level high and bending forward only as much as you need. Though you usually throw your roundhouse kicks to the front, you won't for the purpose of this drill because that uses too much body momentum and hip rotation. Instead, you will kick to the side. Lift your knee and point it at an imaginary target to your side, kick, return to the chambered position, and lower your foot to the floor.

Push your speed with each kick: out, back, out, back as fast as you can. Do 10 kicks with each leg with all kicks.

Partial movements and raw limb exercises not only develop independent limb speed, they also help eliminate any telegraphing that may have crept into your personal style. This happens to even the best fighters and has to be carefully monitored so that it can be eliminated. No matter how fast you become, if you bob your head, sniff your nose, hump your shoulder, or cock your arm, you have eliminated the element of surprise and negated your hard-earned speed.

HIGH-REP KICKING

I have always believed in the value of high-repetition training. I like to think of high reps as an electric sander

Raw-limb kicking uses only the muscles of the leg to launch the kick, rather than momentum. Begin in a natural stance and thrust a side kick as fast as you can, letting your arms hang limply.

moving back and forth across a raw piece of wood, each swipe making the wood smoother and smoother. Indeed, high reps wear down all your bumps, lumps, and splinters so that your techniques flow as if sliding in well-greased grooves.

When done properly, high repetitions will also improve your speed. The act of going through a motion, say the roundhouse kick, over and over strengthens the exact muscles used in the roundhouse kick, particularly the fast-twitch muscles.

Drill 1

I learned this kicking drill years ago from an article written by tournament champion Keith Vitali. It's a tough exercise that will tax your endurance, strengthen your muscles, and, if you push yourself, increase your speed. This is not a drill for lazy people or those who just want to maintain the status quo, and it won't help your speed if you don't push your reps to go faster and faster in spite of the fact that your fatigue wants you to go slower and slower.

There are more than a thousand kicks in this first drill, so the 45 minutes it takes will be more enjoyable if you can get a partner to do it with you.

With a partner, you just square off and take turns kicking at each other, politely pointing out any problems with form or excessive telegraphing. If you train alone, put on whatever music gets you psyched, turn it up, and start kicking the air in front of a mirror. The mirror will provide you with immediate feedback so you can correct any errors and watch for telegraphing problems.

The kicks listed on the following page are ones I like to use, but you can insert any you want. Always include one or two you don't do well and watch them improve with this high-rep drill.

VITALI HIGH-REP KICKING DRILL 1

Single Kicks (Total Reps: 180 Double Kicks)

Technique	Reps	Total
Front Thrust Kick	15	30
Front Slap Kick	15	30
Front Roundhouse	15	30
Rear Scoop Kick	15	30
Front Side Kick	15	30
Front Hook Kick	15	30

Double Kicks (Total Reps: 300)

Technique	Reps	Total
Front Kick, Front Kick	15	60
Side Kick, Side Kick	15	60
Roundhouse Kick, Turning Back Kick	15	60
Roundhouse Kick, Side Kick	15	60
Front Hook Kick, Back Kick	15	60

Supported Side kicks (Total Reps: 100)
If you are doing this drill with a partner, hold hands for balance so that you can chamber your leg higher than normal. Take turns whipping out 50 repetitions; change hands and do 50 with the other leg. If you don't have a partner lean against a wall or hold on to a pole.

Unsupported Side kicks (Total Reps: 100)
This time throw your side kicks without support, relying on your hip strength. Do 50 kicks each leg.

Triple Kicks (Total Reps: 270)

Techniques	Reps	Total
Front Kick, Front Kick, Front Kick	15	90
Roundhouse Kick, Roundhouse Kick, Roundhouse Kick	15	90
Scoop Kick, Roundhouse Kick, Side Kick	15	90

Finishing Kicks (Total Reps: 100)
Select a kick that needs extra work and do 50 with each leg.

There are 1,050 kicks in the drill detailed in the chart. Though I have mentioned several times that you should never push yourself past the fatigue point when you are striving for speed, this drill is the exception to the rule. It's a push-yourself-to-the-max drill, one you should do only once a week or every 10 days. It's strenuous, and you need time to recuperate so that your muscles will grow stronger and faster.

One method of practicing the drill is to begin by executing the first set, single kicks, at medium speed to get yourself physically and mentally into the groove. All subsequent sets should be done as rapidly as possible. The supported and unsupported kicks should be done at full speed or, if you are feeling especially good, at a speed beyond your normal level, red-line speed. The triple-kick set should be fast. The last 100 singles are also done quickly and with good form. As always when doing red line, you want to finish on a positive note with good form and speed.

There are numerous ways to practice this drill. You can vary the pace and the order of the techniques any way you want, but the one constant is that you must push yourself to go faster and faster.

Drill 2

Larry Kelley is another super kicker who was a ranked fighter in the 1980s. He too used a high-repetition kicking drill to develop speed and ultrasharp techniques and wrote about it in the article "Larry Kelley on Kicking" in the October 1984 issue of *Fighting Stars* magazine. The article may be old, but the drill will turn your kicks into a cracking bullwhip.

In contrast to what most instructors advocate, Kelley used ankle weights for speed practice without any harmful side effects to his joints. He points out that the knee is an unstable joint only when it's used improperly. The breaking point for the collateral ligament that binds and stabilizes it is about 5,000 pounds per square inch. Kelly says there is no way you can generate that much force with a kick. In fact, he used 2 1/2-pound ankle weights for three years during a time that he practiced this 1,000-rep drill daily.

Before you supplement with ankle weights, keep in mind that his routine may not have hurt *his* knees, but it just might hurt yours. If you choose to try it, do so progressively, adding a few weighted reps each time you work out. If you begin to feel pain or swelling in your knee joints, discontinue using the weights.

Kelly favors high-speed reps to the head, the theory being that if you build strength and flexibility to kick high, you will be able to kick fast to a low target. Always focus at the point of impact and return your leg as fast as you can.

As with Vitali, Kelly used a 1,000-repetition kicking drill when he was competing. Though this extreme training obviously worked for him, most students may find it too much for them to recuperate sufficiently between workouts. The end result will be muscles that never get completely rested, ultimately resulting in poor workouts and an increased risk of injury.

I still strongly suggest, as I did with Vitali's drill, that you do these high-rep kicking drills only once a week. If you do them more often, you just might find your kneecap spinning across the floor like a loose hubcap flung from the wheel of a speeding car.

The Kelly high-rep drill on the facing page is relatively basic and designed to build strength and speed in the kicks.

If you are quite advanced in your training and physical conditioning, you can start out by doing set one five times and set two twice for 1,000 reps. But if you are a beginner or an intermediate, you probably shouldn't start off with 1,000 reps. You may want to start out by going through the drill just once, which will give you 350 kicks. Then after a month, do set one five times and set two once. After another month or even two months, do set one five times and set two twice, for a total of 1,000 kicks. This may seem like a slow advancement for those of you champing at the bit to progress more

KELLY HIGH-REP KICKING DRILL 2

Set 1 (Total Reps: 100)

Technique	Reps	Total
Roundhouse	10	20
Side	10	20
Hook	10	20
Low Side/High Round	10	20
High Hook/Round	10	20

Set 2 (Total Reps: 250)

Technique	Reps	Total
Roundhouse	25	50
Side	25	50
Hook	25	50
Low/Side/High Round	25	50
High Hook/Round	25	50

quickly, but it will systematically build and condition your muscles for super speed without the risk of over-training and injury.

You can use this basic structure to create your own sets, choosing kicks that are as simple or as complex as you like.

If you train on Monday, Wednesday, and Friday, consider doing either of these 1,000-rep kicking drills on Friday, your last workout of the week. That way you have two days to rest, and you will be fresh for your Monday training.

RETRACTING

I recently saw a video of a karate seminar in which a seventh-degree black belt was demonstrating to a group of students how to sidestep and punch an attacker in the stomach. Every time he demonstrated the move, he would punch out and leave his fist resting against his opponent's chest. Then he either pulled it back slowly or let it drop straight down as if all the energy had been sapped from it. Making matters even worse, his opposite arm hung straight down during the entire punch, as if it was broken or too heavy to be involved in the technique. Not only did he look ridiculous, but he was conveying bad form to lower belts and throwing a punch that could have been much faster and stronger if it had been thrown correctly.

Retracting quickly increases the speed of the attack. The faster the left retracts, the faster the right goes out. The principle that for every action there is a opposite reaction applies here. It doesn't matter where you retract the hand—to the classical position along your side, to your solar plexus as some kung fu styles do, or along the side of your face as do boxers and full-contact karate fighters. But more important than where you retract it to is the fact that you retract it with speed.

It's also important to retract the attacking limb. Never leave it extended except when your mother is taking your photo. Bring it back fast so that there is less chance of your opponent's grabbing it. Interestingly, when you think about bringing it back fast, it goes out more quickly. It's weird science, but true.

Hot-Potato Drills

These drills help you learn to retract your attacking limb. Whether you are a beginner who has not quite got the hang of pulling back your punch or kick after you have attacked or a veteran who has gotten negligent or just plain lazy, the hot-potato drills will get you retracting in short order.

They are called this because the concept is rather like playing catch with a scalding potato just removed from a microwave oven.

Drill 1

This exercise will get you to pull back your hand quickly because if you don't, it will get grabbed. Begin by facing your training partner and assuming your fighting stance. Your partner holds his hands open, palms toward each other and in front of his chest about 12 inches apart.

Your objective is to throw reverse punches at his chest, while he tries to clap his hands together to catch your fist before it retracts. To avoid being trapped, you must snap your punch back. Do 10 reps with each arm.

Drill 2

Obviously you can't retract your other leg when you kick. You can try, but you will fall on your face (really dumb guys will think they did something wrong and try it twice).

The opposite action in a kick is the fast retraction of the kicking leg. For example, when you launch a front kick, it should instantly snap back on the same track on which it went out. But if you just drop it to the floor after it hits its target, you will lose speed and power. The principle is the same as with hand attacks: the faster you snap it back, the faster it goes out.

Face your partner in your fighting stance. Again he stands ready with his hands open about 12 inches apart. When you thrust your front kick at his midsection, his job is to clap his hands against your foot an instant after it touches his stomach. Your goal is to retract your foot so quickly that he can't do it.

These drills can get a little competitive, so be careful you don't punch your partner in the chops or kick him the stomach.

Whether you are kicking or punching in the hot potato drill, the threat of getting your fist or foot grabbed encourages you to attack faster and retract faster. Every time your partner grabs you, you are forced to analyze why and make adjustments. Generally, it's because you are too tense and trying too hard.

DEVELOPING NONTELEGRAPHING TECHNIQUES

Kenpo instructor John LaTourrette says this about telegraphing: "No matter how quick you are, if your opponent knows what is coming, you are not quick enough."

When you concentrate on retracting your punches and kicks with speed, they will go out faster. In this drill, your partner tries to slap his hands on your punch or your kick before you can retract them. Here the punch retracts too slowly and gets caught, while the front kick is snapped back so fast the training partner misses with his slap.

You don't want to warn your opponent of your impending technique. The following drills help you trim all extra fat from your moves.

Drill 1

This is one of the best drills to let you see how much you are telegraphing. It's fun, but be careful because you can easily pop an elbow or a knee joint.

Face your partner, who is holding a hand-held punching pad. Your objective is to backfist as quickly as you can; your partner's job is to jerk the pad away when he sees you move. To hit it, you must make your strike non-telegraphing—that is, no shoulder movement, no hand movement, no twitching of the mouth.

Always remember that movement from nonmovement is obvious, whereas movement from movement isn't. Keep your hands moving so you are not initiating the strike from a static position.

If your training partner is moving the bag away every time you backfist, you need to analyze what you are doing wrong. Ask him what he sees. If you are sending a telegram—twitching, grimacing, sucking in air, belching—stop it.

Drill 2

This competitive drill will reveal any telegraphing signals you may be making before you roundhouse kick.

You and your training partner assume fighting stances and face each other. Your objective is to roundhouse kick him in the hip before he can turn his hip away. You can step up with your rear foot and kick with your front, but a faster method is to scoot forward on your rear foot as you kick. Your partner should tell you if you are telegraphing.

Telegraphing an intention is probably one of the primary obstacles to hitting the target. It's a bad habit that arises from time to time even among the most experienced fighters. It's important, therefore, to periodically check for telegraphic movements in the mirror or throw

When the kicker telegraphs by tugging at her pant leg, the partner pulls the bag away before the kick lands.

techniques at an observant, critical partner. If you can't justify a movement, no matter how small and seemingly insignificant, eliminate it. Your fast kick or punch will be even faster when it's clean, lean, and mean.

CLOSING THE GAP

To effectively hit a good fighter, whether his ability has been earned through training in the martial arts or the school of hard knocks on the street, you must hone your ability to close the gap with speed and deception.

Because your charge across the gap must be explosive and nontelegraphing, it's important to use a stance that works well with your particular physique and fighting style. A basic necessity of a good fighting stance is that you can execute a variety of techniques from it without having to adjust or in some way modify it. If you can only do one or two, you need to get a different stance. The more techniques you can execute without taking the time to adjust your stance, the faster you will be.

For some people that will be the side stance; for others it will be the quarter-turn, boxer-like stance. With either one, the feet must be staggered and far enough apart for stability but close enough together to provide a fast takeoff.

Use Lead-Side Techniques

Most often, lead-leg and lead-hand techniques are going to be faster than rear-hand and rear-leg techniques. The reason is simple: lead techniques don't have to travel as far to hit their targets. On the other hand, they are usually not as strong as rear ones (though some fighters have developed the ability to knock out people with lead kicks and punches). They are good devices to close the gap and set up your opponent for stronger follow-up blows.

Move Arm Before Body

We are going to talk a lot about this in the next few pages. To increase the speed of your lunge, you need to develop the ability to move the attacking limb independently of your body. For example, your jab or backfist should take off before your body moves. If you watch the average karate student, however, you will see just the opposite happen: the body moves forward first and then the hand technique shoots out.

Lead-side techniques are fast because they are closer to the targets. Look how much closer the fighters' lead-side weapons are.

Moving the body first can be dangerous since you are moving into your opponent's range without throwing a technique, leaving yourself vulnerable to an attack. Also, you have virtually told your opponent you are coming after him. Think of it as a massive telegraphing gesture.

If you already possess good speed, independent limb movement will make you faster. If you aren't fast (probably because you haven't finished reading this book), moving the attacking hand first will deliver the technique faster and deceive your opponent into thinking you possess awesome speed.

A fast lead technique occupies time and space, keeping your opponent busy so you can execute follow-up techniques. Think of it this way: if you don't keep your opponent busy with your technique, he most likely will keep you busy with his.

A good lead technique will create an opening for your follow-up blows. When your opponent reacts to your opening lead by blocking, he leaves himself open somewhere on his body, and that is where you follow up fast and furiously.

An explosive lead can knock your opponent off balance. If your opponent reacts to your explosive lead by stumbling backwards or twisting away into an awkward position, take advantage of his weakened stance and hit him with a flurry of hand techniques to drive him back even more. You might even lunge again and foot sweep him onto his butt.

Independent Lead-Hand Backfist

Your lead-hand backfist is going to be faster than a rear-hand technique. As one who firmly believed in economy of motion, Bruce Lee used more lead-hand techniques than rear ones. Certainly, he used more straight-line attacks because they go more directly (economically) to the target.

This is how it's done. Assume your stance and launch your lead backfist. When it's extended about halfway, thrust your front foot forward and drive off your rear leg. When your front foot lands, say 12 to 15 inches forward, your rear foot lands a second later, also 12 to 15 inches forward. That way you are not stretched out to where it would be cumbersome to defend yourself if your attack was blocked and countered. You might argue that you have seen tournament champs lunge out into this stretched position. Unfortunately that's true, but you can get away with it in a tournament where the refs call a

When executing a backfist, the fist moves first, followed by the lunge of the lead foot.

By the time the foot lands, the blow has already struck and retracted.

stop after your lunge. Do it in the mean streets, though, and you just might get poked with a Gerber.

When I lunge with a hand technique, I use the method Howard Jackson used in competition. Jackson, known for his awesome speed at closing the distance, would score with the backfist while his front foot was still traveling forward, retracting his fist by the time his foot came to rest. Karyn Turner in her great book *Secrets of Championship Karate* says Jackson was so fast with his lunging backfist that sometimes you only saw his opponent's head snap back from the blow. Now, I'm not that fast with mine, but I try to have it out and back before my front foot stops moving.

Practice the takeoff over and over, striving for smooth coordination. Once you have achieved it, begin to push your speed using the red-line drill. Make sure your front foot just skims the floor rather than lifts completely off. Retract your backfist before your foot lands and then throw one or more follow-up techniques.

If you are having trouble executing the lunge, don't confuse things by adding follow-up techniques too soon. Wait until you have the lunge and backfist perfected, then proceed.

A Word on Commitment

There is one other important element Jackson, Turner, and other top fighters believe in: total commitment to the lunge. If you are going to charge your opponent with this technique (any technique for that matter), you have got to do so with 100-percent commitment and with all the speed you can bring to the move. You can't get second thoughts in the middle of it, nor can you lunge forward not believing it will work. There is an old saying that applies here: *Whether you think you can or you can't, you're right.* When you think of failure, your body will translate what your mind is thinking. Lunge with total commitment, and you will succeed.

This doesn't mean you attack blindly and with total disregard for your opponent's potential for hitting you.

You are cognizant of what he can do, but when you decide to move, you must do so with absolute commitment to smashing his face with all the speed you can muster. With training and experience, you will find the happy medium.

Let's give the idea of independent arm movement a little harder look.

Bruce Lee and Zorro

One of the most memorable scenes in martial arts cinema takes place in the movie *Enter the Dragon* when Bruce Lee and Bob Wall meet in an arena to fight. The scene begins with them assuming their stances, extending their lead arms, and crossing them at the wrists. There is a dramatic pause as they wait each other out for a few seconds, and then Bruce explodes forward in an imperceptible blur. Wall's head snaps back, followed by his body flying backward as if yanked by an invisible rope. Wall crashes unceremoniously onto his back in the dirt, shocking his character as much as the audience.

"What the hell was that?" everyone asked when the movie first came out. Then a few seconds later, as if to show the audience that their eyes were not playing games, Bruce did it again. But this time the karate students in the audience were watching intently, and what they were barely able to see was the blur of a backfist, its speed and its launch like nothing ever seen before.

Though the movie has been out for more than 20 years, that scene is still as impressive now as it was then. What makes it so is that Bruce Lee executed the backfist with independent arm movement: his fist was out and back before his body had completely moved forward. No doubt there were other fighters using this method back then, but it was Bruce Lee who got the majority of us thinking about it and trying it.

We know Bruce studied a variety of fighting systems, and some people believe that he got the idea of moving the hand before the body from fencing. A quick glance at the mechanics of the fencing lunge shows that the elements are basically the same as for the karate lunge, except for the depth of the final position.

The purpose of the fencing lunge is to close the gap, tag the opponent, and recover quickly so as not to be countered, especially if the attack was parried. In other words, its purpose is no different from that of the karate lead-hand strike.

Let me give you a brief lesson in the fencing lunge; because I'm such a nice guy, I'll give it to you free of charge.

The first step of the fencing thrust is to aim the point of the foil at the exact spot you hope to hit, and, when it is aligned, your arm quickly and smoothly extends from the shoulder. Be sure to relax the shoulder muscles because tension will shorten the reach by as much as one to three inches. Practice this thrust over and over before moving on to the next stage, the footwork.

Now that your arm thrust is moving nicely, you need to coordinate it with a forward step. The mechanics are simple: step forward with the front foot as you straighten your rear leg to drive you forward. Think of the rear leg as a spring, compressed in the on-guard position . . . and then, "boing," it thrusts you forward.

The opposite hand snaps down at about a 45-degree angle behind you. Though this hand position would never do in karate, in fencing it serves basically the same function as a karate fighter's retracting hand: adding thrust to the lunge and helping to maintain balance.

I won't go into the final lunge position because it's far too deep to be practical for karate.

Recovery to the ready position is made by pushing backward forcefully with the heel of the front foot, as your rear leg and both arms return to the on-guard position. It's best to return to the crouched on-guard position because it requires less energy and is faster to assume than an upright stance.

Once you can move out of the lunge and back to the on-guard position with good speed, your next step is to practice scrambling even farther back, as if you were being pursued.

Practice the lunge slowly until you can do it smoothly and flawlessly. Each time you execute a lunge, stop to check your form and make necessary adjustments. Then push for speed; use the red-line drill if you want. Many top fencers practice lunging 100 times per day to keep themselves flexible and increase their speed. Fencers often use a padded target hung from a wall to perfect their accuracy with the lunge, as well as to train their eyes to measure the distance between themselves and their opponents. Once again, they practice the lunge over and over, pushing for greater and greater speed.

Can you see the similarities between the backfist and the fencer's lunge? Bruce Lee did. And he specifically incorporated the independent limb concept with his lead-hand techniques—and did so with extraordinary speed.

Reverse-Punch Lunge Drills

The following two drills will build speed to drive you off the line and nail your opponent with a reverse punch before he can back away. There is no audio or visual stimulus to ignite you in these drills, so you need to psych yourself: turn up the stereo, bang your head on the wall, do whatever it takes to get into the mind-set to explode.

Drill 1

To begin, you and your partner will assume your fighting stances at the normal sparring distance. Your partner should hold his arms wide enough to give you a big, obvious target to hit. Now, relax mentally and physically and get ready to drill him before he can move away.

Using independent arm movement, launch your reverse punch an instant before you push off with your legs. Start the launch from the balls of your feet and drive off your rear leg as you thrust your front foot forward. Although your objective is to lunge and punch, your opponent's job is to back up to escape your charge. If you are fast and able to tag him before he backs away too far, your punch should hit and snap back before your front foot lands.

Drill 2

This is a slight variation of drill 1. Start by squaring off against your opponent, who is holding a striking pad in front of his chest. Your objective is to lunge in as fast as you can and strike the pad before he moves it aside. If you are fast enough, your fist will strike the pad with a resounding smack. If you are too slow or you telegraph your intentions, your big hairy punch will only displace air.

More on Stances

I commented earlier on the difference between static stances and mobile ones, but it's vital to mention it again, especially in this section.

Many traditional karate styles use a static stance, holding frozen postures as the practitioners stare down their opponent and wait for the right moment to strike. The problem is that they are easily detected when they charge forward. On the other hand, motion from motion is harder to see. When you are moving around, varying your arm positions, your stances, or your height, and then you suddenly launch into your opponent, your take-off will be difficult to detect from the other movements you have been making.

Try this experiment. Have your training partner watch as you lunge from a static stance and again from a stance where you are moving. Ask your training partner which lunge was harder for him to detect. Without a doubt, he will say the one that came out of movement. Remember, reaction speed is dependent on a fighter's ability to see a threat, recognize it as such, and respond in some fashion. When you camouflage your lunge with movement, you slow your opponent's ability to perceive and respond, and increase your chance for success.

The speed of your kicks often depends on the type of stance you use. If you favor deep stances, your kicks will be slow because you have to straighten your legs some-what to kick. This fluctuation in height takes time—not much, but enough to where your opponent could hit you first. Why take the chance?

Taekwondo fighters, who kick more than they punch, use a high, nearly straight-up stance; whereas wrestlers, who almost never kick, rely on deep, wide stances. Higher stances allow you to kick easily, as well as move in and out of range with speed and fluidity. But if the stance starts out too high, you will have to come down a little in order to get thrust for your lunge.

The bottom line to all of this is that you will have to find a happy medium with the height of your stance. Find a place where you can kick fast, but that is still low enough to give you defensive stability and lots of spring for your lunge.

Repetition will eventually improve your speed, but so will the right fighting stance. Always stay loose and relaxed on the balls of your feet, maintain movement in your fighting stance, hold your rear fist close to the front side of your body so that it's already halfway to the target, and thrust your hand forward an instant before you drive forward with your legs.

Five Fast Lead Kicks to Cross the Gap

Before we examine good lead kicks, let's look at some that are not so good.

- Spinning kicks, such as back, hook, and crescent kicks, are never good leads because they are too telegraphic and you have to turn your back on your opponent.
- Jump kicks will place you in a vulnerable position when you are in the air and the moment you touch down.
- Dropping intentionally to the floor and kicking upward always puts you at risk.

This is not to say you should never use these techniques. Just don't use them as lead techniques when lunging across the gap. Granted, there are fighters who possess such extraordinary speed that they can get away with doing these things, but such people are rare. Years

The fighter on the right led with a spinning hook, but it's easily blocked and countered with a front-leg shin kick to the groin.

ago, I used to spar with a guy who could lead with a spinning back kick and score with it practically at will. He could do it because he could spin about as fast as Superman spiraling into the ground. But such people are exceptional, and if you are not one of them, use these moves as secondary techniques after you have led with faster ones.

The following kicks are good lead techniques that will get you across the gap fast. Because they are all executed with the lead leg, they are already close to the opponent and require less effort than the larger motion kicks. They are quick and versatile, applicable in tournaments and in the street. In tournaments, however, the scoop kick and low front snap will get you warning calls.

As far as footwork is concerned, I sometimes close the gap by stepping up with the rear foot, anywhere from halfway to all the way to my front foot, and then kick with the front leg. Other times, I scoot forward with the back foot while simultaneously kicking with the front.

Scoop

The scoop kick, sometimes called toe-out kick, is commonly snapped out with the rear leg. It's a little harder to do with the front foot, but with practice you will be able to shoot it out quickly as you cross the gap and finish your opponent with hand techniques. Scoop kick him in the knee or shin and then hit him in the face with punches. I like to kick low and strike high to confuse my opponent, making him think I'm hitting much faster than I am.

Modified Roundhouse Kick

By blending movements of the front kick and roundhouse kick, you make this attack sneaky and hard to block. It travels at about a 45-degree angle straight up from the floor, getting its snap from the knee, which is already somewhat bent in the fighting stance. The target can be either the side of your opponent's knee, inside the thigh, or the groin. Be sure to snap it back for maximum speed.

Front-Leg Snap Kick

I was in Kyoto, Japan, once and watched in awe as a tenth-degree black belt named Sazuki sparred with a half-dozen fifth-degree black belts. He used a lot of front snap kicks, hitting his students in their legs and groin practically at will. I was young then and thought Sazuki kicked that way because he was old and could no longer throw the fancier techniques. Now I realize he used a simple technique because it's . . . simple.

Many tournament fighters don't like front kicks, especially the thrust type, because they have to be too square with their opponent, which overexposes their chest and groin, not to mention subjecting their toes to the risk of getting jammed.

Though these are good reasons to avoid front kicks, you should never avoid something in the martial arts just because others say they don't like it. For example, conventional wisdom has always held that kicks with the front leg are weak, but apparently no one told Bill Wallace, who has turned not just a few opponents into cross-eyed mouth-breathers with his front leg. Don't discard front-leg front kicks from your repertoire until you have given them a good try. They just might be your big point getter.

I like the front-leg snap kick because it's efficient and quick, especially when combined with a fast step-up or rear-leg scoot to close the gap. Because it does lack the power of the rear leg kick, I always choose targets that are vulnerable: shin, knee, inner thigh, and groin. My plan is not to knock the guy down with it, though if he does fall I'm not going to help him up and apologize. My initial purpose is to close the gap quickly and then execute follow-up techniques.

Funny Kick

This is a weird kick that few styles do. I learned it several years ago from a kajukenbo stylist named Sid Lopez, and I wrote about it in an article for *Karate Illustrated* magazine. It's a fast kick, and its trajectory adds an element of surprise. On top of that, it doesn't require the same kind of flexibility as the more common types, so you can kick as high as you want without any pronounced strain on your muscles.

The funny kick requires a combination of a little hip rotation, a sort of outward flipping of the entire leg, and a snapping of the knee. The knee must point straight down

As the next three photos illustrate, the scoop, modified roundhouse, and funny kick are all fast lead-leg kicks. The funny kick is executed by flipping over the lower leg so that the little-toe side of the foot makes contact.

as the lower leg flips the foot out. At the point of impact, the toes are pointing down, and the little-toe side of the foot makes contact with the target.

Side Kick

This kick has a built-in defense if you throw it as described. Assume a side stance and scoot in on your sup-

port foot, chambering your front leg in such a way that the bottom of your foot is pointed at your opponent. This places your chambered leg between the two of you. Take care not to lean back too far because it's not only awkward, but it will be slower to do follow-up things.

Never use a rear side kick for closing the gap. The rear kick may be stronger and you might be able to kick higher with it, but it's too slow compared to the front leg.

The lead side kick will have the greatest speed if you scoot forward on your support leg. This way, both the chambering and the kick take place as you cross the gap toward your opponent, saving you precious time and

making your kick faster. By the time he even thinks about reacting, you have nailed the kick into his ribs. If you are throwing the kick as a fake, hit him with your follow-up techniques the instant he blocks.

CLOSE THE GAP FAST AND HIT FIRST

Who says you have to wait for the bad guy to throw the first punch? Many people are under the impression that they have to wait to be attacked before they can legally defend themselves. When I teach defensive tactics to police officers, I am always surprised at how many think the bad guy has to make the first move. "Hey," I say, pointing at my face, which has been in police work since 1967 and in the martial arts since 1965, "do you see any scars on this mug? There aren't any because I don't wait for the bad guy to move first. I might be having a slow reflex day and not know it until my block misses."

The old adage of the best defense being a good offense is still true, but with a slight variation: the best defense is a *fast* offense."

The old block and counter still work like a charm, but there are times when hitting first will end a confrontation before it gets deadly. For example, if someone is threatening you with a broken bottle, your best defense (providing you are unable to run away) might be to attack with great speed. If a street thug is blocking your way and telling you how he is going break your face, it's in your best interest to attack him first. If someone grabs your arm, do you really want to wait to see what his next move is?

As a police officer who has faced hundreds of people who were crazy, angry, bizarre, loony, emotionally distraught, enraged, or just plain nuts, I rely heavily on my gut feeling. If my instincts tell me this guy is going to go ballistic in the next few seconds, I immediately neutralize him. That is, I move in as quickly as I can and apply a standing control hold, or I take him to the ground if I feel that is the best position. There have even been a few times when I have struck first with my baton when my instincts told me it was the wise thing to do at that moment.

Case in point: I got a call on a deranged man who had just single-handedly destroyed a tavern and was now

walking over one of the bridges that span the
Willamette River in Portland. I found him on the crest
of the bridge and noticed immediately that dispatch had
failed to mention he was 6 foot 5 and 240 pounds. When
he didn't obey my command to stop, but continued to
plod toward me with his arms extended like the
Frankenstein monster, I backed toward the railing and
positioned the cold, gray, swirling river waters to my
back and the steroid freak to my front. Though the guy
had yet to do anything to me other than to glare menac-
ingly as he advanced, I visualized him tossing me over
the railing. I had a decision to make. I lunged at him and
struck his hands twice with my baton. He screamed and
dropped to his knees in agony, and I was able to get control of him after a short struggle.

This was a situation where I was not going to wait and
see what the guy's offensive move was going to be. The
police department doesn't pay me enough to take a swim
with 30 pounds of gear on. Instead, I moved first and sur-
vived to tell the story.

If you make the decision to defend offensively, you
need to do so with speed. You can use any of the techniques discussed in this section to close the gap to punch,
kick, or grab. But you must move with quick footwork,
fakes, and lead-hand and lead-leg moves. This is not the
time to use fancy and complex techniques. Keep it simple and make it fast.

Hitting First When Grabbed

You are justified in using force when someone grabs
your wrist, shoulder, or the front of your shirt. Even if the
attacker doesn't immediately follow up with an assault,
you don't have to wait because the person has already
demonstrated his aggression by touching you and placing
you in fear for your safety. Attack him, but be reasonable.
You are not justified in sticking your fingers in his eyes or
killing him, but you can strike the arm holding you or
apply a grappling technique. On the other hand, if he
grabs you with one hand and displays a weapon in the

other, you don't have to wait and see what he is going to do with the weapon. Use whatever force is necessary, and do it fast.

Stop Hit

This is a simple concept of stopping or jamming the attacking limb so the attack is stopped dead. For example, when an aggressor cocks his fist back, don't wait to see what he is going to do. Quickly thrust your lead hand out and jam his shoulder, and then follow up with a punch. If he starts to kick, jam his leg with your own leg or kick his partially chambered leg and then deliver follow-up techniques.

There is little doubt what an aggressor is going to do when he cocks his fist. However, if the person only moves toward you, the threat may not be as clear. If you are going to go on the offense, be able to justify whatever force you use. On the other hand, if you feel the aggressor is going to attack you, then by all means attack him first—with speed.

In all of these cases, speed is most important: you must move fast to get him before he gets you. Practice your responses as you would any other speed drills. In particular, practice closing the gap as quickly as you can to beat your training partner to the punch. When he chambers his fist, explode into him.

As always, stay relaxed.

DEVELOPING KNIFE-FIGHTING SPEED

I'm going to end this section with a few words about developing speed for offensive and defensive knife fighting. I believe the best way to learn how to defend against a blade is to first learn how to fight with it or, at the very least, learn some basic and realistic offensive tactics. I also believe that as long as I am going to spend the time learning how to use it, I want to be able to execute the techniques as fast as I can. After all, a knife may be the only weapon available in a life-or-death situation.

There is a lot of garbage being taught about knife fighting, theories expressed by people who have never had the sphincter-tightening sensation of facing a cold, sharp blade with their name etched on its side. But there is also good information out there (I have found everything Paladin offers to be streetwise and practical), and it would behoove every martial artist to examine everything on the subject, because second place in a knife fight is usually a bloody place.

Developing speed for knife fighting is just as essential as it is in all other fighting arts. If you are defending against a knife with a knife, you want to get in, do your damage, and then get out before you get cut. The same rule applies if your attacker has a crowbar or 2 x 4 or is an especially good empty-hand fighter. Defensively, you need instantaneous reflexes; offensively, you need explosive speed to startle and overwhelm.

Many of the punching drills throughout this book will help develop knife-fighting speed. The only primary difference is you have a sharp extension to your hand techniques. By the way, this sharpness is a consideration when doing drills that involve the bags. Unless you practice with a wooden dowel or a rubber knife, you will be spending mucho bucks to replace sliced equipment.

No matter what your knife-fighting style, to move fast you must consider the following points when training and when engaged in actual combat:

- Choose a knife that is the right weight for you. That "Crocodile Dundee" blade may look impressive on your hip, but its weight will inhibit speed. You will be able to wield a lighter one much faster, and there will be less stress on your elbow joint as well.
- Breath normally and, as in all fighting, maintain a physical and mental state of relaxed tension.
- Think in terms of cutting or slashing as opposed to making big thrusts. Fast slashing is used to

harass, intimidate, and wear down an opponent before you finish him with a big thrust.

- Gaze at your opponent as if looking far away, rather than focusing on his knife or fist. This will help keep your mind neutral, clear, and more responsive.
- Maintain enough tension in your hand to grip the weapon but keep your arm relaxed so you can move the knife with speed.
- Keep your body moving as well as the blade. Movement from a static stance is easily detected; movement from movement is not.
- Don't waste motion, especially when fighting another knife fighter. While you are posturing and waving your arms around like David Carradine on that stupid TV show *Kung Fu*, the other guy will fillet you to shreds. Eliminate the fat and do only what is necessary.

Most commonly, your defensive and offensive movements will be executed in combinations, at least a block and slash, or a slash and another slash. Before you even begin to practice drills that push your speed, you need to plant the combination in your mind to establish a mind-body connection. Here is a good way to build a solid foundation and get you thinking in terms of moving faster and faster. Use any combination you want: block and slash; slash and slash; block, slash, slash; and so forth.

Begin the movement slowly, repeating it over and over. Some instructors advocate doing hundreds of repetitions before advancing to medium speed. At medium speed you should also do countless repetitions, even when you feel competent to do them faster. Remember, your goal is to establish that mental link that will make the knife part of you. When you are ready for the next phase, and it may take weeks before you are, move on to fast speed. Now, move as fast as you are able and with all the controlled mental rage that would exist in a real fight for your life.

When you practice knife fighting, keep on the move, bobbing and weaving, slashing and thrusting.

Though it sounds mystical, train with these slow, medium, and fast drills until you have "become as one with" the knife. When the weapon has become almost part of you and you are less aware of it, you will benefit more from the other drills in this book that develop perception and reflex speed.

Just as you would never practice a speed drill with a new kick or punch, don't practice with the knife at top speed until you are absolutely ready. Only when you have mentally and physically moved beyond the feeling that you have a foreign object in your hand, should you push for maximum speed.

Creating an Illusion of Speed

The concepts and exercises in this section will make a slow person appear faster and a fast person look even more so. By taking advantage of certain elements of time and space—creative distancing, blitzing, perfect timing, and your opponent's awkward footwork—you will be able to hit with all the advantages that fast hands and feet give you.

I used to work out with a guy who had become quite expert at adapting many of these concepts to his fighting style. When we trained on various karate drills, his speed was about the same as mine, but when we sparred, he consistently tagged me with his punches and his kicks. We even ended up competing against one another in a tournament (Chuck Norris was the center judge, just to name drop for a moment), and he outscored me with what seemed to be superfast punches.

It was sometime later, after I had matured into my analytical phase, that I began to realize it wasn't his tremendous speed that eventually got him listed by *Karate Illustrated* as a top-10 tournament fighter in the region, but rather his ability to use techniques and concepts that made him appear much faster than he really was. By using perfect timing and distancing, he made his average kicks seem to explode into his opponents and his average punch hit like a pile driver. Mother Nature didn't give my friend Bruce Lee's fast-twitch muscles, but she did give him the wisdom to work around that "handicap" and succeed anyway.

Though I call this section "Creating an Illusion of Speed," the illusion is in your opponent's perception. He thinks he is getting zapped with extremely fast kicks or punches. The reality is that you are simply taking advantage of specific concepts and principles of physical combat, which result in the appearance that the techniques are moving with greater speed. We will also examine how these same concepts and principles can be used offensively when facing an opponent who is faster than you.

BE CLOSE BUT APPEAR TO BE FAR AWAY

This concept involves launching your techniques close to your opponent. When you are at close range, your attack has a shorter distance to travel and can therefore get to the target sooner. The trick is to set it up so that your opponent doesn't realize you are close enough to hit him, and then when you do, he thinks he got blasted by Mr. Speed. Sifu Dan Anderson says, "One of the primary illusions of speed is in being so close to your opponent that you only have to move your hand or leg to get him."

Creating an Illusion with the Reverse Punch

Assume your usual fighting stance, but instead of covering your solar plexus with your rear hand, or holding it up near your jaw line, position it forward at the front edge of your waist. Depending on the width of your waist, your fist is now anywhere from 12 to 18 inches closer to the target. When an opening occurs, step in, twist your hips, and launch your punch the rest of the way out. You may even be close enough to punch him without taking a

To create the illusion of distance, throw a few out-of-range backfists.

forward step. Your opponent is left with the impression that your technique hit him with super speed, when in reality it only seemed that way because it moved only a short distance to the target.

Is this punch as powerful as one launched from the far side of your body? Probably not. But in tournaments you only have to hit your opponent hard enough to get a point, and in a streetfight you always want to follow up with other techniques anyway.

Next, cross your rear foot behind you to place yourself within range and surprise him with a smack to the chin.

Notice how I lean back to make my partner think I'm too far away, but look how close my lead leg is to him.

You can use this method of punching as a way to quickly close the gap, distract, and fake. In other words, set him up with a fast appearing lead so you can hit him again, but harder.

Lead-Hand Jab

To its recipient, your lead-hand jab looks faster than it really is because it originates so close to him. Even a jab of average speed will seem faster if you launch it from within range. If you happen to be blessed with a naturally fast one or you have developed a fast jab through training, your speed and the close proximity will allow you to hit practically at will.

Though lead jabs have been basic to fighting since men first began pummeling one another back in the Stone Age, many karate styles don't include them in their repertoire. Too bad, because they are fast and efficient, and they work like a charm to set up an opponent for other blows. If your system doesn't make use of them, take it upon yourself to learn how to throw jabs and then laugh with superiority as you zap your fellow classmates.

Never hold your lead arm still when moving around in your fighting stance. Instead, move it up and down and from side to side. Don't get carried away and do that corny arm-waving stuff that leaves big targets open on your upper body. Be subtle with your hand movements but keep them moving to make it harder for your opponent to detect your attack.

The jab is a versatile technique that can be used as a defensive technique to hit your opponent as he closes the gap toward you, as well as an effective offensive technique to help you close the gap toward him. As Allen Chinn, a kung fu instructor in Seattle, said in the January 1989 issue of *Karate/Kung-Fu Illustrated*, "The front jab is probably the fastest punch there is, so before you begin working on the stronger, combination strikes, you'll want to work on the front jab."

Don't chamber or retract your front jab before you throw it. Instead, keep your arm relaxed and light as a feather, flick it out as quick as a serpent's tongue, and then bring it back even faster.

Some instructors advocate rotating the hand to get additional acceleration out of the jab. Rotation does add acceleration, but consider this: if you are in a real fight and you jab a taller person in the chops, the ridge of his jawbone will probably break your fingers and sprain your rotated hand (this is examined at length in my book *Anything Goes*).

If you insist on punching to a person's hard, bony face, punch with your thumb side up, which positions the first two large knuckles over and under each other. This is a relatively better position that will *decrease* your chances of injuring a hand. In point karate competition this is not an issue, but in a streetfight this slight adjustment can save you some pain.

When training for the street, you might consider jabbing with your palm or gouging with your fingers. Begin from your usual stance, your lead hand unclenched but not open. Jab it straight out and smack your attacker in the nose with your palm or flick his eyes with your fingers.

The relaxed, semiopen hand makes this technique fast, and because it originates halfway to the target, it takes on the illusion of being even faster.

The Sneaky Backfist

This is a technique I learned from Professor Rick Alamany, a kenpo instructor in San Francisco. He has amazingly fast hands and has used the backfist for many years to win the gold in California tournaments. To make it next to impossible for his opponents to defend against it, he likes to couple his fast backfist with the following deceptive way of stepping.

You and your opponent assume fighting stances. Move around and keep his mind busy with your moving hands so that you can maneuver your front foot to the edge of the gap. Throw out a couple of backfists without stepping to convince your opponent that you are too far away to hit him. The third time, cross your rear foot over behind

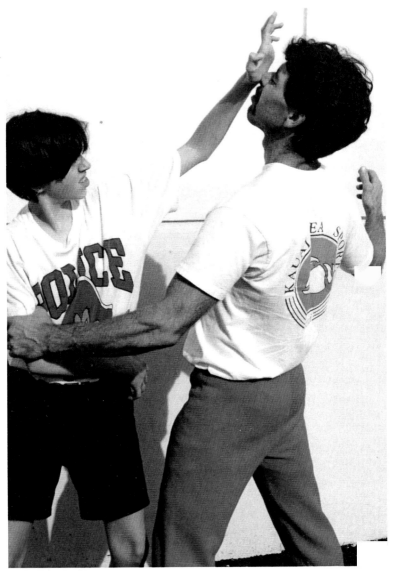

The palm-heel strike is a good weapon to use against a hard and bumpy head, as opposed to punching with the fragile bones of the fist.

As the next two photos illustrate, throw a few far-off jabs to make your opponent think he is safe and then take advantage of his mistake by kicking him in the groin with a modified roundhouse.

your front foot, a move that looks for a moment as if you are falling backward. As you step, launch your backfist. Lo and behold, without stepping forward on your front foot, you have gone from being too far away to landing the technique. Trick-eeeee.

Sneaking in Your Lead Roundhouse Kick

Here is a method of sneaking your lead leg into close range so that you can pop your opponent with a fast roundhouse kick.

Assume your fighting stance, move around a little, and toss out a couple of far-off backfists to make your opponent think you are too far away to hit him. As you keep his attention busy with your hands and lean your upper body back a little to enhance the illusion of distance, stealthily slide your lead foot forward to within kicking range. Then when the moment is right (for example, when your opponent reaches out to block one of your fake backfist strikes), pop a lead-leg roundhouse kick into his thigh or groin.

Don't take the time to chamber the kick. Use the bent knee from your stance, lift your leg into the cocked position (it won't be as tightly cocked as in the traditional way), and launch the kick right into your opponent's inner thigh, groin, or abdomen. As always, snap it back faster than it went out. Then move forward and finish him off or scoot back out of range.

Your opponent is surprised by the kick since your too-far-away hand techniques lulled him into a comfort zone where he thought you couldn't reach him. He was so occupied by your hands that he was unaware your foot had sneaked in close enough to get him. So, unless you tell him it was all done with mirrors, he may never figure it out.

This kick works well in tournaments because it can shoot up at an angle like the modified roundhouse kick discussed earlier, right under your opponent's guard to make a nice slapping sound, drawing the judges' attention to the scoring point. It's effective in a streetfight because you can kick your attacker in the groin to momentarily distract him and then move in to finish.

Deceptive Range

I learned this trick a long time ago from something I read by full-contact fighting champion Benny "The Jet" Urquidez. He suggested that you use a slight up-and-down bounce in your normal fighting stance to trick an opponent into watching your vertical movement and missing your advancement toward him. Then when you bash him with your close-range backfist, he is caught off guard by what he is convinced must be your super speed because he thought you were too far away to hit him.

Knee-Bend Thrust

I got this idea from an article I read in the December 1989 issue of *Karate/Kung Fu Illustrated*. The article was about Chavela Aaron who was then Professional Karate League's and North American Sport Karate Association's number-one heavyweight female competitor. She calls this concept "The Blitz," which doesn't quite define it for me, but what's in a name, anyway? I just call it the knee-bend thrust because that is what you do. The mechanics

Throw a couple of reverse punches that miss by 10 to 12 inches.

of the movement create a deceptive range that gives you greater reach than a regular reverse punch. When you smack your opponent he is convinced you must be a speed demon.

Begin by assuming a shallow-side stance with your feet and body angled just a little toward your opponent. To get an idea of how this technique affects your reach, turn your waist forward and extend your reverse punch. Now, do it again, but this time bend your knees deeper as you rotate your waist and extend your punch. Interesting, isn't it? By just sinking a few inches, your punch extends 8 to 12 inches farther.

*Then without taking a step, dip your knees, lean your upper body
forward a little, and nail him.*

As with the previous techniques, your opponent
thinks you are too far away to punch him. As before, you
can even encourage this impression by throwing a couple
of deliberately short reverse punches to make him feel
safe. Then throw a third punch, this time bending your
knees, rotating your hips, and drilling him in the chest
with the extended punch. As a result of the illusion of
distance, your opponent will once again be convinced
that it must be your killer speed that got him.

Try the knee-bend thrust with a backfist-reverse
punch combination. You can do this in one of two ways

using the same stance as above. The first method is to snap out your backfist without bending your knees and then bend them when you throw the reverse punch. The backfist is used to get your opponent to block; once he has committed himself, bend your knees and hit him with the punch.

The second method is to hit with both techniques. First, throw out a couple of punches to make him think you are too far away and, on the third repetition, sink at the knees and hit him with the backfist and the reverse punch.

Both of these methods will catch him off guard because he is confused by the distance and dazzled by your lightning-quick hands. It's a relatively simple concept that nonetheless requires extensive practice to get smooth and fast.

Drawing

Drawing means you are figuratively pulling your opponent toward you and then hitting him when he gets within striking range. It works like this.

As you are circling and stalking as you usually do, you are going to try to get your opponent to move forward. One way is to shuffle backward a step or two as if you are retreating. Another that works surprisingly well is to wiggle your fingers in a beckoning gesture as you move your hands around. It's a subtle gesture, just enough to penetrate your opponent's brain and get him to respond.

Whatever ruse you use to get him to advance, choose the right moment and abruptly lunge forward and drill him in the chest.

Free tip: In a streetfight, kick the attacker's front leg when he steps forward. It will be close, and his weight will be on it.

The risk with this concept is that your opponent might be well trained and sensitive to range and will hit you first as he advances. Therefore, use this technique only on people you have tested and have determined won't always hit when in range.

As an assailant moves toward you, kick his closest target with your faster and closer leg.

Interrupt His Offense

This works like a charm and will leave your opponent dazzled by what he thinks is your swiftness.

Let's say he is lunging and attacking you with a high punch. When he decides to commit to the technique, he consciously or unconsciously measures the distance he must move to hit you, a distance determined by where you are at that exact moment.

But you are going to interrupt his plan. Just as he moves, step in fast and punch him first. This will disrupt his timing expectation, and because you are so close, you will hit him in one-half to one-third the time he thought his technique was going to take. This will be most disconcerting to him, and he will be convinced your speed is what beat him to the punch.

Moving with Your Opponent
The concept of moving with your opponent requires a high level of skill and will be easier to do when you have become proficient at perceiving your opponent's initial move. The skill you develop at observing partial reps, as described earlier, will help you considerably with this technique.

Know that an attack has three stages: a beginning, a middle, and an end, beginning with the first muscle twitch at the inception of a move and ending when the technique has concluded its course.

Your objective is to move at the first indication of your opponent's technique, not at the middle stage and definitely not at the last stage. In fact, your response should be completed by the time his technique reaches its last stage, if it ever gets that far.

To illustrate, let's say your opponent throws a side kick. He telegraphs his intention by wiggling a toe, pulling at his pants leg, tensing his hip, or curling his lip. At the first indication of the side kick, you should put your response into motion, such as stepping in and jamming his kick, sidestepping and kicking him, or dropping to the ground and tripping him.

To develop skill in this technique, revert to an observation exercise you did in the section on partial reps in Chapter 5. Begin by getting your training partner to slowly throw the side kick at you. At first, just look at the mechanics of the kick: specifically, how it's initiated and what signals are given off before the kick actually begins. Not everyone is going to give out the same signals, so it's a good idea to practice observing several different opponents to note the differences and any signals common to every kicker. Once you are able to recognize them, you can apply whatever response you want.

Let's add a reverse punch, but begin the exercise by just observing it. As before, spend time with several opponents observing just the technique's initial telegraphic movements and then graduate to making a response, such as hand-checking to stop the punch, and countering with a knee into your opponent's abdomen. Remember, to make this concept work you must always make your move in the first stage of your opponent's attack. You move when he moves.

The third stage is to have your opponent throw the two techniques randomly: side kick, reverse punch, reverse punch, side kick, and so on. This is harder when there are two possibilities, so you have to watch closely for the specific signals indicative of the technique being thrown.

The final stage—and this one you will not achieve overnight—is to move every time or virtually every time your opponent attacks. This is the highest level of this concept, and when you have achieved it, you will have honed your skills in perception, timing, and speed.

OVERWHELMING YOUR OPPONENT

Let's look at two ways you can overwhelm your opponent and make him think you are blitzing him with fast techniques. The first method is to rain techniques down on him continuously, never letting up and never giving him a break. The second way is to hit him when his mind is occupied by his poor stance or an awkward movement.

Blitz Him with Your Firepower

This is another of my favorites, maybe because I'm a closet bully. The concept is simple: hit your opponent with everything you have and keep at it until he is reduced to a whimpering infant. The referee says, "Go!" and you attack like a whirlwind. In the street, a thug leaves you no option but to fight, and you attack him like an enraged, frothing beast. The idea with the blitz is to attack hard, fast, and relentlessly. The more he defends, the harder and faster you attack, punching and kicking in a controlled fury. Every beat of time is filled with your techniques, and he is overtaken with speed. Even when you blitz your training partner at slow to medium speed, he will feel that you are throwing techniques faster than you really are. There have been many occasions when I have been sparring slowly with an opponent, and, as I started to blitz at slow speed, he would accuse me of speeding up.

Hit When He Changes Stances

A good time to attack your opponent is when he changes stances; for example, when he moves from a left-leg forward stance to a right-leg forward one. If he is inexperienced, he will be mentally involved with the switch. Even if he is a veteran fighter and makes the change unconsciously, he is still momentarily unstable.

An experienced fighter will change stances out of range of his opponent. He will scoot back a step or two, switch legs, and then move back in. You may still be able to hit him, but you will have to use a fast technique to close the gap. If you have determined he has exceptional speed and skill, it may be best to wait until he is vulnerable in some other way.

If your opponent changes his stance within your striking range, jump on the opportunity immediately. His defenses will be weak as he makes the change, and if he has to think about what he is doing, your attack will momentarily clog his brain and make it even harder for him to think defensively. He probably won't even realize the reason he got hit was because his feet were crossed. He will just think you got him with overwhelming speed.

Some fighters change stances by making a small jump, switching their feet in the air, and landing with their other leg forward. Some do it so fast they feel confident to do it within range. But no matter how fast they are, the switch is still a vulnerable moment.

They often make the switch from a bouncing stance, which makes detecting the movement somewhat difficult, but not impossible. Let your opponent do it a couple of times so you can see what signals he gives off. When you can recognize them, lunge on his switch and cream him.

Another good time to charge is when your opponent is within range and crosses his feet to move sideways. Don't let the opportunity pass. Hit him instantly.

HIGH KICKS OR LOW KICKS?

I have written magazine articles on the impracticality of high kicking, and I dissected it thoroughly in *Anything Goes*. To briefly reiterate: you can't kick high in tight pants, on a wet surface, or in loose gravel, and it's exhibitionism to do it in a short skirt. Also, it just doesn't make a lot of sense to pass by all those good low targets on the way up to a higher, smaller, and more mobile one.

Over the past few years, other writers/martial artists, especially those who train pragmatically, have also given high kicks negative press. Therefore, because so many people have commented on the impracticality of them, I'm not going to harp on the subject anymore . . . except for one last point: you can kick faster when you kick low.

Most martial artists know that there are snap kicks and thrust kicks, and that snaps are usually faster while thrusts are stronger. But both types can be fast when

Sifu Anderson squares off with his opponent.

As the opponent begins to change stances, Sifu Anderson takes advantage of his weak position and distracted mind to attack with a fast backfist.

thrown at an opponent's legs because there is less distance and physical effort involved when kicking low. And because few martial artists and probably even fewer streetfighters can block well with their legs, kicking low is a pretty good idea.

Over my three decades of training, no one has ever come up to me and said, "Wow, do you ever have fast kicks!" Probably because I don't. Sometimes they can be a little tricky, but never fast—except when I kick low.

Even the slightest movement by your opponent will momentarily take his attention from you. Here Sifu Anderson takes advantage of his opponent's lowering front hand to smash him in the face.

I kick low when I spar with people from another school because I love to see their frustration as they try to block my kicks to their groin, thighs, knees, and shins. Because my low kicks have less distance to travel and I can score with them practically at will, my opponents think my kicks are coming faster than they are. Of course, it does help that they don't know how to block them.

If low kicks can make me appear fast, imagine what they can do for a fighter who has already developed fast kicks!

Here are several kicks that can be delivered quickly to low targets. The first four were listed earlier as fast leads to cross the gap. They are that, but they are also great for harassing and distracting.

Scoop Kick

This is a wonderful harassing kick, most effective when scooped into an opponent's knee, though any other place on his leg hurts too. Both the front leg and rear leg kicks are fast, with the front being faster because it's closer. You can either kick and return the foot behind you, or kick, set it down in front, and continue with hand techniques to a high target.

Front Jab Kick

Use the ball of your foot to make contact with this easy-to-do kick. Snap it out from your knee or just snap it from the floor. Use it to jab your opponent in the shin or knee, an especially effective technique if your opponent has grabbed you and pulled you in close. Jab several times in rapid succession.

Front Slap Kick

This kick makes contact with the instep and is most often delivered to the groin, its speed generated by snapping the knee. It doesn't require a lot of power, so just use the knee bend from your stance.

If you are within range, lift your leg quickly and slam your shin up between your opponent's legs. It's quick and low-key, and you can easily follow up with hand strikes to a higher target.

Low Inside and Outside Crescent Kicks

Of the two, the front-leg outside crescent kick is easier to do and faster, though there are fighters who use the inside crescent effectively. The outside kick gets its power from the rotation of the hip and its speed from the explosive snap of the knee. Contact is made with the outside edge of the foot.

The inside crescent, which is usually done with the rear leg and also uses the hip for power and the knee snap for speed, is a little slower than the outside crescent. The point of impact is the bottom of the foot. The best targets for the crescents are the groin, inside of the thigh, and outside of the thigh.

Low Side Kick

You can stretch this kick out and hit your opponent's legs from a considerable distance away, even more so if you have especially long legs. It works well when you sidestep your opponent and blast his knee or thigh. It can be used without a step up or with a quick step or scoot.

Low Modified Roundhouse Kick

This kick is faster when you don't chamber it first. Use whatever bend you have in your front leg from your stance and straighten it in a snapping fashion as you launch your foot on a path to your opponent's inner thigh or groin. Snap it back faster than it went out and kick again if necessary. This is one of my favorites because it's so hard to block.

Low Hook

When executed as described, this sneaky little kick will appear to come out of nowhere. The idea is to shoot your lead foot out along the floor, hook your opponent's front foot, and upset his balance.

It's not as quick as the others, so you have to camouflage its entry. Keep your opponent's attention distracted with your hands as you inch your foot forward right under his nose and hook him before he realizes it. To make it look as if you are too far away to do anything, lower your stance and lean away for a moment before you hook him.

The low hook works defensively as a surprise counter to a high punch. When your opponent steps in, you simultaneously block his attack and hook his forward leg.

As opposed to kicks delivered above the waist, all of these kicks can be delivered with less time, effort, and telegraphing of intentions. Low kicks will definitely get you a warning in competition, but they will frustrate your sparring partner—or any street attacker.

Free tip: When you step up with your rear foot to close the gap prior to a front-legged kick, you will save time if you set your stationary foot with the toes pointed away from the direction you are kicking. For example, when you step up to execute a side kick, set your stationary foot anywhere from 90 to 180 degrees away from the target. This lets you get the technique off much faster and keeps the stationary foot from having to twist on a surface that has a lot of friction. I once broke a knee when my leg wanted to turn but my foot got caught on a sticky floor.

SPEED WHEN BLOCKING AND COUNTERING

When you are attacked, your opponent is mentally anticipating that his blow will land at a particular moment. The following blocking and evading techniques will disrupt your opponent's thought process because of the speed of your counter.

Some of the following methods are more efficient than the usual block-and-counter approach because they save actual time. Some work because of the illusion of distance they create.

Simultaneous Block and Counter

When your timing is right on the money with this block-and-counter concept, your counter will hit at the same time your opponent is expecting his blow to hit.

For example, say your opponent launches a reverse punch at your head. Swat it aside with your hand and simultaneously punch him in the chest with your reverse

Setting your stationary foot prior to kicking is safer for your knee joint and faster because it eliminates friction drag on the floor. Assume a fighting stance in preparation for a turning back kick.

Move your hands around to camouflage your foot placement prior to kicking with your right leg.

punch. This can be disconcerting because his brain is anticipating his blow to land at the exact moment your blow hits.

Your block and counter must occur at the same time. Just as there is no such thing as almost pregnant, there is no such thing as almost simultaneous. Almost any attack can be blocked and countered in this fashion as long as you are close enough to reach the attacker.

Close-range attacks should be countered with close-range techniques. For example, when your attacker grabs toward your neck with one hand, block it and simultaneously drive your elbow into his chin. If he grabs your lapels with both hands to pull you into him, respond by smashing your fists down on his upper forearms as you drive your knee into his groin.

Middle-range attacks should be simultaneously countered with middle-range techniques. For example, a reverse punch can be countered with another reverse punch, a backfist can be blocked and simultaneously countered with a punch under the attacking arm, and a roundhouse punch can be blocked as you drive your palm into the attacker's chin.

Though kicks are generally considered long-range techniques, you can use a short-range kick to block a middle-range attack, such as a shin kick to your opponent's groin as you block his head punch or a snap kick to his shin as you block his middle punch.

Long-range attacks are easily countered simultaneously with a kick. You will find when any one of the five basic kicks—front, round, back, side, and hook—is delivered groin high or higher, you can quickly counter with a front slap kick underneath. For example, as your opponent launches a side kick at your middle, block it aside with your arm as you sidestep and pop your front leg up into his groin or to the underside of his attacking leg.

Blocking and kicking simultaneously is especially disconcerting to an attacker who likes to kick head high. I like to counter low against a high kicker because his attention is as high as his foot. As he thinks about my

A simultaneous counter is fast and surprising. When an attacker grabs this woman, she responds at the same instant with a side kick to his leg.

forehead, I think about his shin. The simultaneous counter surprises him and shifts his thought process down to his leg. I then follow up with a high punch, confusing him even further. When he raises his hands, I kick him low again. At this point, most people just give up in frustration because my techniques appear to be coming fast and furious.

Is there power in a simultaneous counter? Of course, though probably not as much as with a counter that is able to build more momentum after a block. But then, as has been said many times in this book, you should hit more than once anyway. Think of the first counter as one that surprises the attacker and sets him up for the rain of harder punches and kicks that follow.

Because simultaneous blocking and countering doesn't provide you with the best body mechanics to hit with great power, consider countering to vulnerable targets, ones you don't have to hit hard to cause pain and distraction. For example, block his head punch as you simultaneously gouge his eyes. By hitting vulnerable targets, you will distract an attacker's attention long enough to give you time to follow up with other techniques.

Same-Hand Block and Counter

The concept behind this is almost the same as that of the simultaneous block-and-counter drill: a fast response that bewilders the attacker. It does this by taking advantage of the position of your blocking arm, which is generally closer to the attacker than the non-blocking arm.

Say your opponent throws a jab at your face. You slap it aside, being careful not to overextend the block, and then hit with a backfist with the same hand. The counter is quick because your hand is already involved in the technique, placing it at least halfway closer to the attacker than your other hand, which is probably chambered somewhere alongside your body or beside your chin. This relates to the axiom about the shortest distance between two points being a straight line.

You can also apply this method when blocking a kick with your leg. For example, when your training partner launches a front kick to your groin, lift your leg and block it, and then immediately snap your foot into his groin. The response is quick because your foot is already chambered and perfectly positioned to kick back. It won't be a powerful kick because your foot is too close and there is no momentum behind it. But it will set him up for other blows.

As the next two photos illustrate, blocking and countering with the same hands saves time and energy. Sweep block the attacker's reverse punch and immediately slam him with a backfist.

Try the concept when you block a kick with both hands, such as when you block a roundhouse kick to your left side with your left arm, and augment the block with your right palm. Because your body is twisted slightly to the left, your right hand is closer to the attacker and on a direct path to his groin. Simply snap your right hand out and score.

As with a simultaneous block and counter, this counter won't be your hardest blow, but it will take your attacker by surprise because of its speed.

Go through your blocks and determine what you can and can't do with your blocking arm. You won't be able to counter with every block immediately because your position won't always be right for it. But when it is, it works like a charm.

Blocking without Blocking

Blocking with the hands and legs is basic in all martial art schools, though most students and instructors would rather spend the time working on offensive techniques, especially fancy, fun ones (in all too many schools blocking is not emphasized as much as it should be). Think about this for one quick second: if you can't avoid getting punched or kicked, the only fancy thing you will be doing is lying on the floor, listening to the blood dripping out of your ears.

Blocking is important, to understate the point. You may get away with simply charging in with your attacks in sport karate, but in the street, where knuckles are not protected by foam rubber and feet are covered with everything from running shoes to construction boots, blocking is a necessity.

Many martial arts systems teach that the epitome of blocking is not to block. That is, the superior fighter evades by ducking, bobbing, weaving, and twisting away. I'm not sure if I would agree that doing such things makes a fighter superior, but developing skill in evading will provide you with several advantages:

- It keeps your blocking arm from getting injured.
- It frees both hands and both legs.
- It leaves you in a good position to counter fast.
- It positions you to counter simultaneously.
- It saves energy.

I like evading an attack because if I can position myself right, I can counter fast, either simultaneously with my opponent's attack or an instant before his attack lands. I can't do it with every attack, but when it works it's effective and disconcerting to my opponent—and it looks cool.

As with everything else in the martial arts, evading takes practice and a certain amount of conditioning. So instead of just jumping right into the various evasions, you should first practice the exercises listed below to help you understand the movements and to condition the muscles involved.

As you practice with your partner, keep in mind where you are in relation to him. The better your position—the closer you are to him when you evade—the faster your counters will land. But on the other hand, you have to be careful because if you are too close, you won't be able to evade in time. Let's take a look at the ways you can evade and how to develop skill and speed of execution.

Ducking

Strong legs are required to lower your body quickly and return to your upright stance with speed. Squatting exercises are probably the best thing you can do to develop the exact muscles involved in the movement.

1. With your hands on your hips, squat slowly and concentrate on feeling the muscles work in your thighs and around your knees. Do three sets of 10 reps.
2. Begin this exercise with your hands on your hips. Squat down quickly and then spring up. These reps should be pumped out quickly to develop speed and explosiveness. Do three sets of 10 reps.
3. As your training partner swings a stick at your head, duck under it at maximum speed and spring back quickly, as if you were countering. This not only develops your fast-twitch muscles, but works your reflexes as well.

Small Head Evasions

To develop the ability to avoid a punch or kick to your face, you need to practice turning, tilting, twisting, and bobbing your head. These are small, quick movements that can be made quicker with the following simple exercises.

1. Practice slow rotations of your head, feeling the muscles work in your neck and shoulders. As you turn as far as you comfortably can to the left and right, keep looking to the front, as if you were keeping your eyes focused on an opponent.

2. Loosen the muscles of the neck by shaking your head from side to side, rotating it clockwise and counterclockwise, and moving it up and down. Use caution with the up-and-down motions so that you don't go too far and strain your neck muscles or injure your spine. Keep your eyes trained on the imaginary opponent to the front.

3. Have your training partner throw medium-speed high punches. Your objective is to use whatever evasive movements are applicable to keep you from getting hit. Your partner should punch progressively faster as your ability improves. Always keep your eyes on your training partner as you move.

Body Twist

Your ability to twist your body to either side will help you avoid punches, kicks, pushes, and grabs. Many aikido and jujitsu experts can do it with such speed and smoothness that their lunging attackers find themselves grabbing nothing but air.

1. Put your hands on your hips and twist your body from side to side without moving your feet. Do it slowly, concentrating on loosening your hips and waist.

2. Assume the same position as you did above, but this time snap your waist and hips as if avoiding a fast grab. Twist enough so that your entire body is turned sideways to the invisible attacker and, as always, keep your eyes on him.

3. Have your training partner throw medium-speed kicks at your upper body as you twist to

By quickly leaning your head away from a punch, you are in place to counter with fast punches of your own.

avoid them. As your skill improves, progressively pick up the speed.

Jumping

Jumping is probably best left to small, agile fighters, though it's a good way to evade if an attacker is swinging a stick at your feet or kicking at your ankles. If you are putting on a demonstration, leap as high as you can, but if you are in a tournament or a street fight, jump only high enough to avoid getting struck. It's also a good idea to jump in such a way that you can counter on the way down or immediately after you land.

1. The rapid squats used in the ducking section are good for building jumping speed as well.
2. Jumping rope develops the ankles and calves. On every fifth or tenth jump, spring high with both legs.
3. Stand next to a low object and jump up and over it. Practice jumping forward, sideways, and backward.
4. Get your training partner to swing a stick at your ankles. Jump up and come down countering.

As the next two photos illustrate the defender twists away from the push so that he can quickly whip a clothesline strike across the attacker's neck.

7

Defending against Speed

So what can you do if you have a confrontation with a guy who has read this book before you and is now faster than a teenager avoiding hard work? What can you do to neutralize his rapid charge, quick backfist, or snapping roundhouse kick? What if *he* catches *you* by surprise?

Below are several methods of defending against a fast attacker. Learn them and experiment with them in a variety of situations and with numerous training partners of all sizes and shapes.

SACRIFICE BLOCKING

In *Anything Goes*, I debunk much of sport karate, in particular, a method of defense I call sacrifice blocking. For example, say your sparring partner throws a head-high roundhouse kick at you. To sacrifice block, you would lean back a little and take the kick on the side of your shoulder. To sacrifice block a chest-high side kick, you would position your arms vertically in front of your upper body and take the kick against your forearms.

You can get by with these blocks virtually injury free when your opponent is wearing foam-rubber sparring boots, but they can be painful in a street confrontation when the attacker is wearing heavy cowboy boots.

As I warned in *Anything Goes*, if you sacrifice block in competition, you will be conditioned to block that way in a real fight. Though this is still true, there are times when sacrifice blocking is your only option to keep from getting hurt worse. Examples would be when an attacker catches you off guard with overwhelming speed, when you are attacked at close range and you have your arms full of groceries, or when you have your back to a wall. If you practice sacrifice blocking only under these conditions, you won't risk developing a habit of doing it under normal fighting conditions.

You need to keep yourself covered whenever you are facing an opponent in competition or in the street. If the attacker, whether fast or slow, is close enough to hit you, keep your defensive guard up: your hands near your face and your forearms and elbows close together. This position keeps your upper body covered, thus making you a harder target to hit. But there will always be gaps in your defensive wall, and for sure those gaps will be what a fast puncher will go for.

If a punch comes so fast that you can't get off a regular block, you will have to sacrifice block to save yourself. Since your arms are already in front of your upper body, simply move them to the opening. By absorbing the blow with your arms, you are protecting your upper body, while looking for a way to counter.

Absorbing padded punches on the forearms is no big deal in tournament competition, other than conditioning you mentally to do it all the time. If karate is just a sport to you, and you don't care about such negative conditioning, go for it. But if you are studying karate for self-defense as well as sport, be sure to do extra training with regular blocks after the competition is over.

Sacrificing your forearms to a bare-knuckle punch is harsh reality in the street, but it's the lesser of two evils.

Will the blows be painful? Ain't no doubt about it. Will you save pain and destruction to more vulnerable targets? Yes.

Protecting Your Lower Body

You have only one groin, so protect it, no matter what.

If you are not already doing so, consider turning your front knee inward a little in your fighting stance to protect your groin against a surprise kick. But there are still some sneaky kicks that can snake around your knee and bite you, and there are fighters who have the speed to move quickly to a different angle to get around your leg guard. When one of these things occurs too fast to block, turn your knee in a little to cover your groin. Granted you will take the kick on your knee, but you will protect a more vulnerable target.

You can also use your leg to jam a fast kicker. Simply lift your knee, usually your forward one, and absorb his kick on your shin, leaving your hands free to block or counter in the event he follows with fast hand techniques. Make sure your weight is inclined forward so that the impact doesn't knock you backward and so that you can lunge and counter with less effort.

Sacrifice blocking is a tool to use when you don't have time to execute checking- and deflecting-type blocks. When you are forced to sacrifice block, your arms and legs will get struck painfully and may be injured, but you will have avoided getting struck with a fast punch or kick to a vulnerable area that could debilitate you and prevent further defense.

In a perfect world, you would fight so well that the emergency conditions that require sacrifice blocking would never occur. But in case you haven't noticed, it's not a perfect world, and stuff happens.

MONITORING THE GAP
WHEN FACING A FAST OPPONENT

I can still remember my first instructor, Bruce Terrill, founder of the Oregon Karate Association, telling the class over and over to stay out of the gap unless attacking or countering. In the late 1960s, this was somewhat innovative because so many fighting systems were sparring literally lead hand to lead hand. Though most schools now teach the importance of maintaining distance unless attacking, it's easy to get lax at times and stand too close.

Though you should always pay attention to the gap between you and your opponent, it's never more important than when you are fighting someone fast, especially someone faster than you. Always keep in the back of your mind the fact that because he is fast, he can cross the gap in a split second and drill you. And if you happen to wander into the gap without attacking, the last thing you will see is your fast opponent's smile.

How Far Is Enough?

The best way to determine the minimum gap between you and your opponent is to visually measure the extension of your opponent's rear-leg, front-thrust kick. This is a distance basically the same with everyone, with the exception of especially tall or short fighters.

Closing the Gap on a Fast Fighter

Let's say you are up against a fast fighter who scrambles backward like a quick rabbit every time you move against him. Here is a little trick that often works.

Take a step forward with your lead foot to see how far he backs up. If it's just one or two steps, that's good. Do it a couple of times to establish a pattern in his mind and to put him into a comfort zone where he believes you are not going to advance any further. The third time you step forward and he steps back, say hello to him in his comfort zone by lunging forward once more and backfisting his surprised face.

Your add-on step can be a lead-leg lunge, a rear-foot scoot, or a replacement step. Use whichever one gets you across the gap as quickly as possible.

Keep Moving

I have mentioned several times in this book that you should not maintain a static stance, but rather stay mobile. This is especially important when facing a fast opponent. Why make it easy for him by standing in one spot and letting him pick you off?

Move continuously. One moment you are in a right-leg, forward-side stance, the next moment switch to the left-leg forward stance, and then into a quarter-turn stance. Your arms are moving back and forth and up and down, and he doesn't know if you are attacking, faking, or just moving erratically. You want to keep him on guard so that he has to think defensively rather than offensively.

Keep the fast fighter wondering what you are doing and where you are going to be. Take the fight to him.

8

The Grappling Arts

My grappling experience has been mostly in jujitsu and police defensive tactics, so I will be referring to them frequently in this section. However, the following exercises and drills are applicable to all the grappling arts—jujitsu, judo, aikido, wrestling, chi'n-na, hapkido, police defensive tactics, and others. They can be used as described or modified to fit the specific needs of your particular art.

Keep in mind that response speed is still response speed regardless of the fighting art. First, the eyes must perceive a stimulus—be it an attack or an opening—and send a message to the brain; the brain must assess the information as a threat or an opportunity, scan the possible responses available to it, and then send a command to the appropriate muscles to do the right thing. That is a given in every fighting art, though the type of response depends on the art. It could be a block and kick, jumping backfist, hip throw, or bullet in the attacker's face.

All this to say that many of the drills already described can be used for a grappling response. It doesn't matter what the stimulus, as long as it sparks the grappler's

Police officers use grappling techniques against resisting suspects every day. Here an officer applies the "face crush" to get an uncooperative suspect to see it her way.

reflexes and sets him off like a swirling tornado flattening homes in a trailer park.

If you train in an art that is a combination of karate and some form of grappling (count your blessings because the combination of the two is the smartest approach there is to practical street self-defense), go back through this book and look at the drills you may have previously seen as applicable only to the punch or kick arts.

Use your imagination and creativity to see how they can be modified to fit your grappling techniques. For example, a reflex drill using the punching pads can be changed so that you grab an imaginary opponent's arm in the air and then strike the pad. Or you might respond with a strike to the pad first and then follow up with a grabbing technique in the air. Release your imagination, get creative, and you will find most of what you thought were just karate drills can be modified to grappling drills.

If you only practice the grappling arts or police defensive tactics and you skipped to this section of the book first, again I suggest you look at the drills described on previous pages to see which ones apply or can be modified to fit your needs.

A Word to the Traditionalists

Keep an open mind as you study the following exercises and drills. I say this because there are some grappling arts—usually traditional aikido, judo, and jujitsu systems—that look upon ideas outside their system as blasphemous to the ways the old masters taught (read *Anything Goes* if you care to hear me rattle on about closed-minded martial artists). Approach the following with an empty cup and give the concepts and exercises an honest chance, even if they are in disagreement with your current beliefs. If you do so, one thing for sure will happen: you will become a faster grappler.

Why Do You Need Speed in the Grappling Arts?

Don't you just grab the guy and throw him down on his butt? Yes, you do, but the operative word in that question is *just*. You don't *just* do it; you do it with surprise, sneakiness, stealth, distraction, and lies, all of which adds up to one thing: *speed*.

In many grappling classes, the opponent stands motionless and lets you choke his neck, flex his wrist, trip his leg, and bend his elbow in a direction so painful that only Satan could have invented the move. Though it's true that your opponent must stand still while you learn how to apply a technique, grappling schools often continue to practice in this fashion long after the move has been learned. This instills a sense of false confidence in the student because the opponent or street mugger certainly isn't going to stand still.

Police Defensive Tactics

One of the glaring weaknesses in most police defensive tactics programs is that officers train only at the initial learning stage, slow to medium speed. Few programs allow their officers to practice at maximum speed. There are lots of reasons for this: time and budget constraints, the administration's concern about officer injury, and lack of knowledge on the part of the instructors on how to teach speed. The number one reason, however, is that many officers, especially those who have been on the job for a while, refuse to put out the effort. To those I say good luck. To the officers who want the tactical edge and to develop greater speed, read on.

CLOSING THE GAP IN GRAPPLING

For a grappling technique to work in competition or in the street, you must successfully close the gap (in the grappling arts this is often called *entering*) and then apply a technique so fast the opponent or attacker can't resist you. Closing the gap successfully means you have got to enter with speed faster than your opponent can react defensively.

Independent Limb Speed

When I talked a few pages back about lunging with the backfist or lead jab, I said that to move at maximum speed, you must lead with your hand and then follow with your body. This is because moving your body first telegraphs your intentions, whereas moving your hand first is harder to detect since it's small and faster.

Independent arm movement is a technique used often when entering to grapple. For example, say you want to enter to choke. Begin the technique by thrusting your lead hand forward toward your opponent's closer shoulder, and at the halfway point drive forward with your legs. Slam your palm against your opponent's shoulder, spin him around, slip that same arm around his neck, and apply whatever choke you like. The independent arm lunge can be used when entering to quickly apply an arm lock, hair hold, head twist, or any number of other techniques where the lead hand is used to immediately apply a grappling hold.

The lead arm can also be used to distract or fake your opponent. For example, thrust your palm at your opponent's face and, when when it's about three-quarters of the way there, shoot your body low to his legs for a tackle. The fast fake creates a distraction and a startle reaction in your opponent's brain, giving you time to attack elsewhere.

Police Defensive Tactics and
Independent Arm Movement

A large percentage of police officers are hurt and killed in the early stage of a making a physical arrest. Your verbal skills (aka, b.s. ability) and your entry speed will dramatically increase your success at gaining control of a suspect. Independent arm movement is an effective way to move with speed.

Say you have been interviewing someone and have gathered enough information to make an arrest, but the subject is edgy and volatile, and you feel he is going to run or fight when the arrest is attempted. He has yet to be aggressive toward you, so a softening technique is not justified. You must somehow close the gap as quickly as possible, take his arm, apply a control hold, and react if he resists.

As always, keep in mind that the subject, and any onlookers, may complain of police brutality if your action appears too aggressive. It has been my experience,

*The police officer snaps her arm out first and then drives forward
with her legs to close the gap before the suspect can run or fight back.*

however, that when an officer applies techniques with
speed, skill, and professionalism, people are less likely to
snivel of brutality, including the bad guy.

Moving the arm first and driving forward with the legs
will quickly get you across the gap, where you can apply
whatever control hold fits the situation. It's so quick that it

Every time the defender tries to execute a leg sweep, the attacker presses his weight forward.

minimizes the opportunity for the subject to resist, which of course minimizes the potential for a fight or complaints.

If your defensive tactics system has five grappling techniques, analyze each to determine how to use them with independent arm movement to cross the gap.

The next two photos illustrate that the defender "softens" the attacker with a strike to his throat to drive him back and set him up for a leg-sweep takedown.

SOFTENING

I know a few jujitsu holds that can twist and tie a guy up so much that he looks like a pretzel on LSD. But I also realize that to apply them in a real fight, I would first have

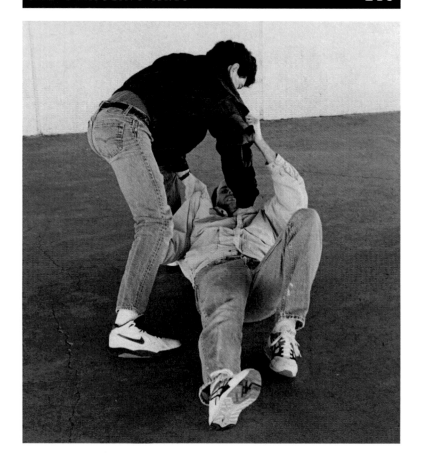

to beat the guy in the temple until his skull was concave enough to make a good birdbath. Thumping the opponent before applying a grappling technique is called *softening*.

If you apply an armlock on your opponent too slowly, chances are he will stiffen or jerk his arm away. Of course, a veteran grappler will be able to flow into a plan B and use his opponent's resistance against him, but other martial artists—such as karate students who have only a small repertoire of grappling techniques—may not be so versed. Softening is a good device for them.

Let's say you and a street attacker are jostling about in a clinch. Your plan is to pull his arm down, step up to his side, and use your closer leg to sweep back against his to

The next two photos illustrate how police officers should avoid getting into muscle contests with suspects. When the suspect strains to get away, the officer distracts him by driving her knee into the highly sensitive peroneal nerve in his upper thigh. The shock of the blow will slow his resistance and quickly allow her to apply a control hold.

take him down onto his back. This is a technique as old as the hills and commonly called by its Japanese name, *osoto geri.*

But every time you go for it, he stiffens and leans forward, either because you are sluggish with the setup or because he is simply faster than you. It's time to soften him up. This time when you move to his side, slam your forearm across his Adam's apple instead of draping it across his chest as you did before. When his eyes bug out like those of a mountain hiker who has stumbled upon a nudist camp, you sweep his leg.

Police Defensive Tactics and Softening Techniques

Most police agencies don't allow softening techniques like the one just described, unless you are in a survival situation where anything goes. But not all is lost because there is something you can do that is a little like softening and a little like distracting.

Let's say you are standing alongside a suspect and begin to apply a wrist lock, but he stiffens his fist into brick hardness. Now what? You are not allowed to gouge his eyes or chop him across the neck to soften him (wouldn't it be easy if we could, though?). But you are justified in using a milder form of softening.

When a subject stiffens his fist or arm, you should always consider it a form of resistance. Why is he doing it? Is he just frightened, or is he setting you up for an attack? Since you don't know and you don't get paid enough to wait to find out, you must move to establish control. Because he is mildly resisting, you are justified to soften him with a pinch to the inside of his upper arm or a jab to his ribs with your thumb. This will cause him to flinch and distract him enough to apply a wrist lock.

This entire process is done very quickly. You grab the suspect's arm; he resists; you execute a quick softening technique and apply the control hold. It is low key, done quickly and smoothly, and leaves the bad guy with the impression that you are one quick cop.

To execute a fast knee-tug takedown, first fake high to your opponent's face.

FAKING

The purpose of faking is to redirect your opponent's mind elsewhere to give you an extra second or two to enter. By the time his attention returns to you, you have already got him.

Say you and your opponent are squared off, stalking each other, looking for an opening. When the moment is

Immediately drive your head into his abdomen as you tug behind his knees and dump him on his back.

right, use independent arm movement and thrust your hands toward his head-neck area, as if going for a head twist or a choke.

He will react to your gesture in a number of ways: he may lean back, brush your arms aside, side step, or shuffle backward. It doesn't matter to you—you are going to abruptly change direction, thrust your head into his abdomen, and simultaneously reach around his knees to jerk his legs out from under him.

You were successful because your fake directed his attention high so that your real attack could move freely to a low target.

Police Defensive Tactics and Faking

There are ways you can fake and distract to facilitate moving in on a subject. The idea is to manipulate his attention and implant an expectation in his mind. When the subject has been faked or distracted, you have given yourself a moment, however brief, to apply the real technique.

Try this subtle method of faking when you enter to take a noncombative subject's arm. As you cross the gap toward him, gesture face high with your fingers as if beckoning him to step forward. As you move in, simultaneously say something like, "Come here. I want to talk with you." As the subject's eyes look at your wagging fingers and his ears listen to your command, quickly take his arm. The gesturing fingers divert his attention to a high place while you reach to a midlevel spot. This is not done at great speed, but to the subject it seems quick because his attention was distracted.

Crossing the gap to take a suspect into custody can be dangerous. Here the officer gestures with her fingers to the suspect and says something like, "Come here. I want to talk to you," as she crosses the space and reaches for his arm. His mind is momentarily filled with her gesture and her words, allowing her time to move in.

Here is a technique I have used several times when entering against a resistive subject who has twisted his body away from my first reach. The next time I move, say toward his left side to take his arm, I assume he will twist away again. If he doesn't, I'll take that arm. But if he does, he will inadvertently turn his right arm toward me. Since I'm not picky, I grab it and apply whatever technique fits the situation. This always makes them mad, but deep down I think they are really impressed at how fast I seem to be.

Look at your grappling techniques and determine how you can use independent arm movement, softening, and faking to facilitate closing the gap between you and your opponent or suspect.

Always think in terms of speed when you enter, whether it's actual velocity of movement or the execution of a concept that creates a sense of speed.

UCHIKOMI

Uchikomi is a Japanese word that refers to the practice of moving in on an opponent. Sensei Tim Delgman, a high-ranking jujitsu instructor with the Zen Budo Kai of San Francisco, calls uchikomi "a body-fitting drill" because of the way the defender fits his body into an attacker's body. Here is how it works.

Say an attacker moves toward you, striking downward toward your head with his right fist, a technique somewhat common in street fights. To defend with a grappling technique, you would block his arm with your left arm, pull it down as you step forward to his right side, and thrust your right arm across his chest. You would then swing your right leg forward and bring it back to sweep his leg as you simultaneously tug downward on his arm. It's the ol' osoto geri again.

To practice uchikomi, you would execute only the first phase, stopping short of taking your opponent to the floor. You would block the attacking arm, pull the arm down to his side, step along the same side, and kick your sweeping

Sensei Tim Delgman practices uchikomi by stepping into his opponent, squatting below his center, and stopping just prior to the throw.

leg behind him. Some instructors teach that you should stop where your leg touches the back of his, whereas other schools stop the technique even before you move your sweeping leg behind him. I have my students stop at the point they feel the sweep has their opponent off balance.

Delgman stresses high reps with the drill, 25 to 100, always striving for proper "fit" so that the defender's body moves into the exact place to execute the completed move. He stresses high reps so that the entry becomes automatic, smooth, flawless, and fast.

He also teaches escaping from the entry. Say you are defending yourself in the street with osoto geri, but as you step in everything goes wrong. Maybe the attacker is faster than you, or you slip on the wet sidewalk or enter incorrectly. Perhaps you are in competition, and your opponent starts to execute a reversal against you. Tim Delgman believes it's important to practice fast retreating so that you can escape a hot spot before you are countered.

Delgman says that to be beneficial, all movements in uchikomi must be done correctly with all unnecessary movement eliminated. Precise "bare bones" movement itself will increase your speed. Repetitious practice of uchikomi will make you even faster.

Solo Uchikomi

You don't always have to practice uchikomi with a partner. Practicing solo is a good alternative when you are alone or healing from an injury. Pick one or two techniques and practice them for 30 minutes, pushing yourself to move faster and faster as your rep count goes higher and higher. Because you don't have a partner to discuss technique with, your practice can go uninterrupted, making it a great cardiovascular exercise.

To develop speed in uchikomi, pay attention to the following points:

- Practice only those moves you are familiar with. Only correct practice will help you improve.
- Concentrate on being "light" and fast.

- Do no fewer than 25 repetitions. If you are advanced, do 100 reps. Remember, you can't develop speed when you are tired. Here is a way to slow the onset of fatigue: you perform 10 to 20 reps, your partner does 10 to 20, you do another 10 to 20, and so on.
- Start at medium speed and build to all-out, red-line speed.
- Practice with partners of different heights and weights.
- Try to explode into your partner without telegraphing.
- Recognize when you are having problems with a technique. If it can't be immediately corrected, stop uchikomi practice so that you don't ingrain incorrect technique.
- When your partner is doing uchikomi on you, don't resist. By resisting you will interrupt his flow and ultimately interfere with his speed development.

Uchikomi with a Finish

One could argue that too much uchikomi might hinder your ability to complete the entire move. I don't know, but I suppose it could be argued that if all you practice is entering, you might stop at that point in a real fight or in competition.

To benefit from the entering drill and to keep the total movement complete in your mind, simply add the takedown portion of the technique in every fifth rep. So, if you are doing a set of 25 reps, you execute five completed ones. And just to make sure your mind is in the right place, finish your drill with 5 to 10 completed techniques.

Uchikomi and Police Defensive Tactics

Police administrators are always concerned about their officers getting injured in training, especially in defensive tactics. Most police officers are not martial artists, have no idea how to fall, and are not used to getting their arms wrenched and their feet swept out from under them. As a result, it's not uncommon for officers to receive minor injuries in training. Uchikomi is an excellent training device for police officers, not only because it helps develop smoothness and speed of technique, but because it minimizes the chance of injury.

Let's look at how uchikomi can be used with the arm-bar takedown, a common technique found in many police defensive tactic programs. Say you are standing on the suspect's right side holding his right arm, your right hand on his wrist, your left hand gripping just above his elbow. To apply the technique, your right hand turns his wrist so that his palm is up, locking the elbow, and then your left forearm presses against the point just above his elbow. You then pull up on his wrist and push down on his upper arm until the subject is bent over at his waist, he pivots, and you prone him out.

When practicing uchikomi, you won't complete the arm bar by taking him to the ground; rather you stop when he is bent over and off balance. You get the benefit from practicing entry, and your opponent is saved from skidding across the mat on his lips.

As I said earlier, many officers are injured when making contact with subjects who don't want to be contacted by the police. There are two times when an officer is most vulnerable. One is when he crosses the gap to make initial contact. The other is during the transition between holding onto a subject's arm and the first phase of a pain-compliance hold.

Practicing uchikomi with police applicable techniques is one way to develop skill, smoothness, and speed in both of these highly vulnerable areas.

BE LIKE A MIME

There ought to be a law that lets us hunt mimes. Just one short month out of the year, we could go to Central Park in New York or just about anywhere in San Francisco and shoot them with a crossbow.

But before we hunt them all down, let's steal their art of pantomiming and see how it can benefit our speed in grappling.

I was preparing for my second-degree black belt test in jujitsu at the same time that I was teaching beginners how to take falls. Initially, there were a couple of young guys eager to please me who stayed after class to let me smash them to the floor. But their eagerness quickly waned, and they began disappearing in a puff of smoke immediately after the class ended.

Left without opponents, I had no choice but to create them in my mind. In fact, at least half of my training time was spent pantomiming the movements, exactly as I would do them with a live partner. I would pantomime a block, entry, grab, and execution of the takedown and finish, which was sometimes a lock and sometimes a punch or kick. I practiced dozens, sometimes hundreds of repetitions in this manner. Later, as my test date grew near, I would grab a student in class and coerce him into letting me do the techniques on him. After making some adjustment to live body weight, I was able to do the techniques on him as if I had been practicing with a real person all along.

A most important consideration when pantomiming a complex or even a simple grappling technique is that you do it *exactly* the way it is done with a real partner. That is, don't leave out even the slightest nuance; pantomiming does not mean doing the technique vaguely.

When I pantomime jujitsu (always in the privacy of my home or school, never on a street corner or in a shopping mall), I not only practice every physical detail, but I add emotion, intent, and controlled rage. I also push to go faster and faster, which improves not only my speed but my cardiovascular system as well.

To enhance speed, I practice uchikomi. I practice moving in over and over, emphasizing driving with my legs as fast as they can move, cognizant that my hands, arms, and body are doing what they are supposed to be doing. After 5 to 10 reps, I move on to the takedown, do another

5 to 10 reps, and then move to the last phase, which is either a lockup or a strike.

Pantomiming grappling techniques is a great way to train when you can't get a partner or when you want to supplement your regular training with something a little different. You will find that you can push your speed more with your imaginary friend because you don't have to deal with real weight and resistance. Realistically, when you do the technique against a live body, you won't be able to do it at the same speed as in the air. On the other hand, it just might be faster than if you had spent the same amount of time practicing on a live opponent.

Pantomiming Part of a Technique

With this concept, you pantomime just part of a grappling hold. Unlike the last drill, where you executed a technique from beginning to end, here you concentrate your efforts on whatever part of the technique you want to work.

To illustrate, let's practice a concept from arnis called *chain hand*. Assume a fighting stance with your left leg forward and visualize a right punch rushing toward your face. Sweep it away with your left hand, catch the invisible wrist with your right, hold on to it, and then shoot your left arm across his chest to knock him over backwards. Repeat the move over and over, concentrating on keeping your muscles relaxed as you push your speed faster and faster. Do it on both sides for balanced training.

DEVELOPING GRABBING SPEED

Without grabbing speed, you aren't going to do a heck of a lot of grabbing. No matter how many holds you know, you need hand speed to grab your opponent's arm, leg, neck, or whatever.

Hand speed, particularly finger speed, is essential in the grappling arts. If you lack the speed to close your fingers around an opponent's wrist before he pulls away, you have lost that all-important moment in the martial arts known as "The Opportunity."

With the exercises that follow, you can increase your hand and arm speed dramatically, plus you will increase your hand and finger strength.

Four Fingers to Thumb

Touching your four fingers to your thumb is done as if you were picking up an object with all five fingertips pressed together. Repetitiously open your hand and spread your fingers as wide as you can and quick as a wink bring them all together. Your goal: 180 reps in 30 seconds.

Fist Clenching

Fist clenching involves opening your hand as wide as you can and then closing it quickly and tightly. Your goal: 180 reps in 30 seconds.

Finger Curling

Curling your fingers to your palm is done by curling first your index finger and then each finger in order until all five have been curled into a fist. Your goal: 150 reps in 30 seconds.

Two-Finger Drill

The last exercise is done by spreading your thumb and index finger as far as you can and then bringing them together as fast as possible. Your goal: 180 reps in 30 seconds.

You must do these exercises as fast as your fingers can move. Do each exercise for 15 seconds at first, increasing to 30 seconds in about two weeks. Try to do around 180 reps in 30 seconds; the record is 300 reps in 30 seconds! Do the first exercise and rest for 20 seconds; then the second, and rest for 20 seconds; then the third; then the fourth. Pause for 30 seconds and repeat the cycle again. Do three cycles, keeping your hands relaxed by shaking them out when they get too tight.

There is nothing complicated about these finger-closing exercises, and they can be done just about anywhere. I like to do them in the morning while driving to work. By the time I make the 15-minute trip my forearms are so pumped they feel as if they are going to burst through the skin. As a result of doing them for about a year, my grip (which has always been wimpy) has grown stronger, and my grabbing speed has improved twofold.

Reach and Grab

In this drill you will combine the finger-grabbing movement with a reaching movement. Begin by relaxing and visualizing an opponent reaching toward your chest. Snap your hand out and grab the imaginary arm, clenching your fingers around it as fast as you are able. Repeat the movement 10 times with each arm.

Lunge and Grab

This time you will coordinate your hand-grabbing and arm-reaching speed with your lunge. Your arm will move first, of course, followed by a powerful lunge with your legs. Your grab should be complete by the time your lead foot lands.

Defensive Tactics and Grabbing Speed

Police officers are seldom taught how to grab the bad guy with speed. As mentioned before, budget limitations and administrators' concern about injury to officers dictate that police defensive tactics are generally taught by having officers stand cooperatively in static stances as they take turns twisting each other's wrists. Problems arise, however, when that trained officer goes to apply a control hold on the street and discovers, to his chagrin, that the bad guy doesn't stand still the way his training partner did.

Practicing defensive tactics in the air and drilling on rapid finger-closing and speed-grabbing exercises are ways police officers can train without risk of injury and without costing their agencies additional money for training. I know from experience that these methods will keep their techniques sharp and help develop the speed needed to apply them in a combat situation.

SPEED GRAPPLING DRILLS

The following drills, which can be used in any of the grappling arts, will develop reflex speed and movement speed. They have been used for years in collegiate wrestling, judo, and jujitsu, and are as fun to do as they are potentially rough.

Side-by-Side Drill
You and your training partner lie parallel on a mat. Stay relaxed so that your response is fast on the audio stimulus. A third person, say the instructor, blows a whistle, claps his hands, or in some other way makes a sharp, audio command. On the sound, you both attack each other using grappling techniques, stopping on the instructor's command or when one person has been pinned or controlled. This is a reflex drill, so your response to the command stimulus must be explosive.

Top-of-Head to Top-of-Head Drill
This is basically the same drill as the last one, except that you and your partner start out lying on your backs, your legs going in different directions, the tops of your heads nearly touching.

On the audio command, you both explode into action, turning as fast as you can to pin or control your opponent.

Back-to-Back Drill
This is similar to the other two, except that you start in a seated position, your backs pressed together. On the audio command, you both twirl and grapple.

In all three of these drills, you need to maintain a relaxed tension as you await the command and then move fast and explosively when you get it. The competitive spirit of the drill encourages you to move with speed.

Where you go with it after the audio command is up to you. Sometimes you might battle until someone applies a pin or a control hold, or you might just go at it for 10 seconds and then stop.

Police Defensive Tactics
and Speed Grappling Drills

These same drills can be used in defensive tactics, as described above, or modified so that they are more applicable to police work. It's important that they be closely monitored by the instructors to prevent injury.

Several years ago, I experimented with an academy class using speed grappling drills. I had the recruits start in a clinch, as most police-suspect skirmishes do; when I shouted, "Go," the recruit acting as the arresting officer had to burst into action and get control of the resisting suspect.

After only two sessions, one officer had been rushed to the hospital with a split forehead, a wall had been ripped loose, and several clocks had been knocked from the walls of an adjoining district attorney's office. I was ordered to stop the drills.

GETTING UP FROM THE FLOOR WITH SPEED

When you are standing and facing an opponent who is standing, that is one thing. When you are down on the floor grappling with an opponent who is also on the floor, that is another thing. But when you are down and your opponent is standing, that is a bad thing. If you are knocked down in a fight or in competition and your opponent is still standing, it's critical that *you get up quickly.*

Here are some drills that will encourage you to scamper to your feet with speed.

Whack-'Em-with-a-Stick Drills

These could also be called reward-and-punishment drills. I learned them from jujitsu black belt Tim Lynch, student of Sensei Dave Sumner, head instructor with

Jujutsu of Oregon. They are fun exercises, but only if you are successful at them. Allow me to elaborate.

Drill 1

Begin by standing on a mat in a relaxed ready position, facing your instructor, who is holding a long stick at the ready. When he swings the stick at your chest, drop straight down onto your back in a break fall or drop and flow into a backward roll. In either case, immediately get up and assume your fighting stance.

Drill 2

This time fall onto your stomach when the instructor gives you a verbal command. The moment you hit the mat, he charges in with a fast downward strike with his stick. Because his intent is to hit you, it's in your best interest to get out of the way quickly and back on your feet.

Drill 3

Here is a variation on the first drill. Again the instructor swings the stick at your chest and again you drop backward onto the mat. But this time when you land, the instructor is on you like a fly on you-know-what, striking downward with the stick. Your job is to quickly roll, scoot, or spin out of the line of the stick's downward trajectory and get back onto your feet and into your fighting stance.

The instructor should not chase you with the stick. The drill is to encourage you to get up or at least not to stay where you fall. You should always get up or scramble away quickly, so that a competitor or a street attacker can't get you with follow-up techniques.

Police Defensive Tactics and Whacking

Slipping or getting knocked to the ground is a highly vulnerable position where you could get kicked, beaten with some kind of a weapon, or even shot. Of course, whenever you are in a weak position, you are at risk of losing your sidearm and having it used on you or on innocent citizens. It's imperative that you get up as quickly as possible.

You should practice the whack-'em-with-a-stick drills in the same way as illustrated above, except for one major difference: always get up with your gun side away from the attacker.

TOUCH REACTION DRILLS

The following are good drills to enhance your sensitivity to touch and to build a speedy response to it.

It's never a good idea to let anyone grab hold of you. A puncher will grab your arm while he pummels you with his fist. A grappler has to grab you before he sends you hurtling into space or before he chokes you like a chicken. No matter what kind of fighter is grabbing you, you need to escape fast and respond with a fast counterattack.

Back Touch

This is a fun drill that will spark your reflexes and keep you jumpy for several minutes after. Begin by turning your back on your partner, closing your eyes, and relaxing. The moment he touches your back with his fingers, immediately turn and catch his hand.

As your skill increases, your partner should touch you more and more lightly and to different parts of your back—shoulders, upper spine, lower spine, left side, right side, left hip, right hip—and he should always snap his hand back after he makes contact. When you get consistent at catching the light touch, you know your reflexes have become responsive and fast.

Respond with a Grappling Technique

This drill will help you develop a fast, reflexive grappling response. How and where you are touched is up to you and your training partner.

Say your partner reaches toward your shirt front, a rather common technique prior to pushing, pulling, or

You must practice to respond immediately to an aggressor's touch. Here the man on the left grasps the collar of the man on the right.

The defender quickly steps in, pivots, and throws the aggressor onto his head.

throwing a punch. Don't wait to find out which it's going to be. The instant you are touched, grasp your opponent's hand, step away from his free hand, and execute a joint lock or takedown. If you want to add a softening technique as you go for his grabbing hand, feel free.

Close Your Eyes

With this variation, your eyes are closed to heighten your sensitivity to touch. Stand ready and relaxed as before. The instant you feel it, snap your eyes open, grab his hand as fast as you can, and apply a hold or takedown.

Practice your response over and over so that you have no hesitation in your movements. Remember, the longer you wait, the more time the attacker has to follow up with a second technique.

In the following touch-grab drills, your training partners can help you progress by first reaching slowly toward you. As before, your goal is to try to react before the initial touch turns into a completed grab. Once you are reacting consistently at slow speed, your training partners should reach a little faster. Continue in this progression until you able to react with great speed.

Line Drill

This variation of the touch drill is used by jujitsu sensei Tim Delgman. Begin by assuming your fighting stance as you face a line of fellow students, all of whom are itching and twitching to get at you.

The first one charges forward and attacks with a random grabbing technique. Your job is to respond defensively with a joint lock or a takedown the instant you are touched. When you finish with one attacker, the next one charges. Continue in this fashion until you have gone through everyone in the line. Your emphasis is on an immediate and fast execution of a response to the touch before it can turn into a grab. As always, push yourself to move faster and faster.

Circle of Death Drill

This time the attackers encircle you. This is a little harder than the straight-line drill because some attackers will be rushing at you from behind. Stay relaxed but ready and don't anticipate which attacker or which attack will be coming. Remember, when you anticipate incorrectly, you can't react with ultimate speed because you have to take time to stop your wrong thinking and replace it with correct thinking. Keep your mind clear so that it can think of only the correct response.

As each attacker moves in, strive to move so fast that you react before the touch becomes a grab. Apply a locking technique or a takedown and be alert for the next attacker.

Delgman offers this speed tip that is especially valuable when training with the circle or any time you have to defend against multiple attackers: "The sooner you see an attack, the faster you can respond to it. It's important to develop your peripheral vision so you can more quickly see an attacker who is off to the side of your direct vision."

Police Defensive Tactics and the Touch Drills

As a police officer, you need to develop an immediate response to a threatening touch before it turns into a grab. You can only assume when a suspect grabs you by the arm, shoulder, or shirt front that he is up to no good. Don't wait to see what the definition of up to no good is. You must respond immediately and with all the speed you can muster. Always step to the side away from his free hand and, whenever possible, position your weapon away from him. What you do at that point is up to you, the situation, and your department's policy. Some departments may not consider a grab threatening enough for you to respond with a hand strike or kick. Therefore, you would have to execute a grappling move. Whatever you respond with, do it as quickly as possible.

Since most officers are not martial artists and have a limited repertoire, the instructor should limit the response in the touch drills to just one or two techniques. For example, stand normally and look straight ahead while your partner stands off to your side. When you are touched on your arm, shoulder, chest, or neck, immediately turn toward the threat and apply an arm-bar takedown.

Most grappling techniques require the element of surprise to be successful, and, without a doubt, extraordinary speed can be a big surprise. When a grappling technique is delivered with lightning-quick speed, the opponent doesn't have time to block, evade, counter, or stiffen up. But the development of such speed takes work, energy, and sometimes pain. But it's worth it.

Things
to Think About

Here are a collection of tidbits gathered in the process of researching this book. Read them and chew on them for awhile because there is substance in each one. Ask yourself how they relate to your particular martial art and your development of speed.

- Three elements will make you faster immediately: deception, relaxation, and independent arm movement.
- Maintain a physical and mental state of relaxed tension.
- Fatigue will slow your reaction.
- "If you practice very hard, you will be very good."—Remy Presas.
- You are a stick of dynamite. When you move, explode.
- "The stronger your legs, the harder you can kick and the faster you will move when closing the gap between you and your opponent."—John LaTourrette.
- "Think" your stance light.

- "The only thing that goes through my mind is how quickly I can beat my opponent."—A judo champion.
- When punching, concentrate on relaxing your shoulders.
- "When executed well, leg techniques should appear to pop like serpents from some dark, unseen, open pit, and their strikes should be as astonishing as they are effective."—Eric Lee.
- Anger and fear will prevent you from moving with great speed.
- If you are not paying attention, your reaction will be poor.
- To create the illusion of speed, time your attack to hit your opponent as he moves into you.
- "Find an attitude of loosening antagonistic muscles prior to delivery, a continuous waiting attitude rather than a preparatory one."—Bruce Lee.
- When your opponent attacks, respond instantly with your own attack while your opponent's is still on the way.
- Straight blows travel less distance and hit their targets first.
- "Think" of yourself as already being fast.
- Before practicing kicking drills, mentally remove all the tension from your pelvic/hip area.
- When throwing a backfist, snap your wrist forward on impact and then snap it back. Think of it as snapping a towel.
- Retract your kick faster than it went out.
- Strong muscles move faster.
- Relax your muscles, not your thinking.
- Flexible muscles move faster.
- The faster your punch comes back, the faster it goes out.
- Move slowly at first and then add speed as the movement becomes natural.
- "Your blow should be felt before it is seen."—Kenpo axiom.

- A big person doesn't always indicate a slow person.
- To react with speed and accuracy, maintain a clear mind and don't anticipate your opponent's attack.
- Fast action and fast reaction are two different things and require different training exercises.
- Persevere and great speed will be yours.
- Train for balance while training for speed and you will never kiss the floor.
- Dodging exercises should be designed for you to get out of the way, stay balanced, and position yourself to counter with speed.
- "Think" your legs as light as a feather.
- When thrown correctly, the backfist gives no warning and just possibly might be the fastest hand strike.
- "Snapping the kick [rather than thrusting it] is not only a safer kick on the knees, but a quicker method too."—Bill Wallace.
- Both speed and skill are handicapped by tension.
- Finger flicks to the eyes are quick as a blink and require no focus of the arm muscles.
- Eat for speed.
- "When a fighter spots an opening or has put an opponent on the defensive, he needs speed to take advantage of the moment."—Steve Sanders.
- Make your opponent think you are fast.
- "One of the most important moments in every tournament match is the initial move."—Chuck Norris.
- Hit when he changes his stance.
- Lack of commitment will get you punched out.
- A good lead attack is economical, fast, and creates an opening for follow-up blows.
- The harder you try, the slower you will move.
- To develop speed, you must practice specific speed drills two to three times a week.

- In the development of speed, you also develop power.
- Work out with fast training partners.
- Bedazzle your opponent with the speed of your techniques.
- Strike fast to "tenderize" your opponent before applying a grappling technique.
- In a side stance you can evade a blow more quickly.
- Work to reduce the time between your block and your counter.
- When throwing combinations, reduce the time between hits.
- Whether you think you can or you think you can't, you're right.
- "The more you practice, the better you get."—Kathy Long.
- Don't try too hard.
- Economy of motion reduces telegraphing and increases speed.
- "I am fast."—Three words you say to yourself throughout the day.

Conclusion

As I write this conclusion on a chilly November day, I'm about halfway into my 30th year of training and teaching in the martial arts. Until I began writing this book four months ago, I thought my progress in the fighting arts had pretty much peaked, at least physically. I knew I would continue to learn and gain knowledge until the day the Grim Reaper hacked me with his scythe, but as far as making any big strides in speed and power, I had accepted the conclusion those days were over.

But I made a happy discovery writing this book: I had been wrong. Incredibly, as I experimented with all the exercises and drills, I began to see my speed improve. Even at the graying age of 48, my techniques were beginning to get faster and faster. My good arm was snapping out techniques as quick as a whip, and my kicks, my forever slow-as-a-slug kicks, were starting to crack the air faster than ever before.

Part of this improvement was from training in the drills I have illustrated in this book. And I worked them all: perception, reflex, audio, visual, movement, weight training, and the many others listed for each aspect of speed development. But as much as I sweated over them, I'm convinced that at least half of my improvement has been from just thinking about speed over the past few months.

"What did he say?" inquires the lazy reader. "This guy got faster from just *thinking* about getting faster?"

Well, sorta. The concept of speed has been a constant in my mind for the past several months. I thought about it, I visualized it, I researched it, I talked to others about it, I trained for it, I watched fast fighters, I taught the drills, and I simply thought of myself as getting faster and faster.

When I trained, I trained with the confidence that I was going to get faster. The end result: after a few months I got faster.

Am I as fast as the many experts I talked about in these pages? No, but I'm definitely faster than I was a few months ago, and what is really exciting is that I'm not as fast as I will be a few months from now.

About a month before I finished writing this book, I saw a newspaper article about a guy who was going to give a demonstration of quick-draw and speed-shooting techniques. I knew these guys are fast so I went to take a look.

The shooter that day was Bob Munden, and he calls himself "the fastest gun who has ever lived." Oh yeah, you say. What about those cowboy guys who used to meet on a dusty street in some no-name town to have a speed-draw showdown? Munden said that never happened. Such scenarios are totally a fabrication of Hollywood writers.

Speed drawing/shooting is a modern-day sport, and Munden holds 18 world records in it. How fast is he? The *Guinness Book of World Records* has timed Munden's draw at less than one-half of one-tenth of a second, less time than it takes an eye to blink.

I watched his demonstration, and I still can't believe what I saw. He stood next to a box that had a large light bulb on its top. When the bulb would light, that was his

Bob Munden, "the fastest gun who ever lived."

cue to draw and shoot a hanging balloon a few feet away. He could do it so fast he beat my blink every time, usually before my eyes were even half shut.

He didn't use a breakaway holster, either. He pulled the .45 all the way out, pulled the hammer back with either the shooting hand or his opposite hand, shot the balloon, and even holstered before I could blink.

He could shoot two balloons six feet apart so fast the shots sounded like one. He could shoot a semiauto and then shoot the ejected shells before they hit the ground. His hands moved with such speed it was beyond visual perception and mental comprehension.

After his demonstration I asked him how often he trained. He said his shows keep him in good shape, so he doesn't practice as much as he used to. But early on in his career, he would practice 3,500 repetitions of drawing the weapon and shooting every four days. That doesn't count the number of draws he made when he didn't shoot. Amazed by the number, I asked how his competitors trained. "They would do about 200 draws," he said.

When I asked what his mental approach was to his art, his answer was the same as so many champions in other endeavors: "When I go into a competition," Munden said, "there is no way I can lose. I am absolutely convinced that no one is faster than me, and there is no one who can beat me."

As I drove home that day, still in awe of Munden's imperceptible hand movement, I thought about how martial arts training compares to what he does.

He believes in high-repetition practice, and so should you, though I would never recommend doing 3,500 kicks or punches every four days. High-repetition practice will ingrain a martial arts technique into the subconscious mind, so that later you will reflexively respond to a block or an opening faster than what your conscious mind can process. Additionally, high reps will figuratively smooth the bumps and splinters on all the body parts involved, so that the move will flow smoothly and with great speed.

Munden's conviction that he is fast directly affects his physical actions. If he didn't think he could move that fast, he couldn't. Call it confidence, call it will, or call it acceptance of what he perceives as fact. But because he knows he can move fast, he can.

If you *believe* that you will become faster, that you will develop speed far greater than you have ever imagined—you will. Know it in your head and your body will follow.

The mental and physical exercises in this book depend on each other. You can make some gains just by taking the mental approach, and you can make some gains just by doing the physical drills, but when you combine the two, you will open a treasure chest.

Good luck.